HIGH VISTAS

HIGH VISTAS

❧

An ANTHOLOGY of NATURE WRITING
from Western North Carolina & the Great Smoky Mountains

VOLUME I • 1674–1900

George Ellison
Illustrations by Elizabeth Ellison

natural

HISTORY
PRESS

Published by The Natural History Press
A Division of The History Press
Charleston, SC 29403
www.historypress.net

Cover design by Marshall Hudson.
Cover image: These Mountains, Elizabeth Ellison.
All illustrations by Elizabeth Ellison.

First published 2008

Manufactured in the United Kingdom

ISBN 978.1.59629.355.7

Library of Congress Cataloging-in-Publication Data

High vistas : an anthology of nature writing from western North Carolina and the Great Smoky Mountains
/ edited by George Ellison.
v. cm.
Includes bibliographical references.
Contents: v. 1. 1674-1900.
ISBN 978-1-59629-355-7
1. Natural history--North Carolina. 2. Natural history--Great Smoky Mountains (N.C. and Tenn.) 3.
North Carolina--Description and travel. 4. Great Smoky Mountains (N.C. and Tenn.)--Description and
travel. 5. North Carolina--History, Local. 6. Great Smoky Mountains (N.C. and Tenn.)--History, Local. I.
Ellison, George, 1941-
QH105.N8H54 2008
508.756--dc22

2008016090

For
Fred Houk
(1951–2007)
&
All Those Who Also Cherish These Mountains

CONTENTS

CONTENTS

PREFACE

I started haunting rare and used bookstores when I was attending the University of North Carolina at Chapel Hill in the early 1960s. Though my inclinations in regard to both collecting and reading have varied through the years, my primary area of interest has always been that far-ranging branch of literature that can be generally categorized as "nature writing."

When my wife Elizabeth and I moved with our children in the early 1970s to Bryson City, North Carolina, on the southern boundary of the Great Smoky Mountains National Park, it was inevitable that I would focus my attention upon nature writing that depicted in one way or another the southern Appalachians. I quickly realized there was a wealth of materials that, for the most part, few people had access to or even knew about. To help remedy that situation, I initially envisioned an anthology that would present selections having to do with the mountainous portions of Virginia, Tennessee, Georgia, South Carolina and North Carolina. It didn't take me too long, however, to realize that such an anthology would require numerous volumes. So I retreated and narrowed my target area to the region I know best.

This is the first anthology devoted to the nature writing of Western North Carolina and the Great Smoky Mountains, inclusive of the Tennessee side of the present-day Great Smoky Mountains National Park. Arranged chronologically with biographical essays and annotations, the twenty-one selections in this first volume display the variety and development of writing in this genre for over three centuries, up to 1900. That story will be continued into the twenty-first century in a second volume of *High Vistas*, scheduled for publication in 2009.

With the exception of late nineteenth-century writings by ornithologist William Brewster and travel writer Bradford Torrey, very little in this first volume qualifies as what many modern-day readers would necessarily define as "nature writing." The various selections could just as easily be categorized as descriptive, travel, out-of-doors or adventure writing. But these are the sorts of diverse materials and perspectives that form the basis for the natural literature of any locale. From 1900 to the present, Western

North Carolina and the Smokies have been closely observed and quantified by some of our finest nature writers, including Horace Kephart, Donald Culross Peattie, Roger Tory Peterson, James Fisher, Edwin Way Teale, Harvey Broome, Edward Abbey, Harry Middleton, Christopher Camuto and others.

In this first volume there are selections from the writings of well-known authors such as William Bartram, André Michaux and John Muir. But most feature the work of lesser-known authors whose voices deserve to be heard. The reader will find firsthand descriptions of mountain flora and fauna, geology, topography, forests, rivers, waterfalls and high vistas, as well as depictions of the lifestyles and lore of the Cherokees and mountaineers. Searching for rare wildflowers and elusive birds, scaling vertical cliffs, experimenting with medicinal plants, exploring a vast cavern, enduring horrific thunderstorms and encountering timber wolves, panthers, black bears and giant rattlesnakes are some of the adventures that unfold in these pages.

The focus herein is on nonfiction prose. Well-known nineteenth-century travel writers like David Hunter Strother ("Porte Crayon"), Constance Fenimore Woolson and Rebecca Harding Davis, although of considerable interest, are not included in this anthology because they chose to fictionalize their accounts.

Most of the biographical essays that accompany the selections originally appeared in two publications. In 1993, Dr. J. Dan Pittillo asked me to contribute a quarterly "Botanical Excursions" column to *Chinquapin: The Newsletter of the Southern Appalachian Botanical Society*. Through the years, Dan—who recently retired from the Biology Department at Western Carolina University and passed along the editorship of the newsletter—was an excellent editor, as well as a good friend and supporter. In 2000, I started contributing a weekly "Back Then" regional history column to *Smoky Mountain News*, a newsmagazine published in Waynesville and distributed in the North Carolina counties west of Asheville. Editor Scott McLeod and his staff are to be commended for their efforts in producing this valuable regional publication. All of the essays in this anthology have been entirely rewritten and, in most instances, expanded.

We first got to know and trust the staff at The History Press when, in 2005, they published my *Mountain Passages: Natural and Cultural History of Western North Carolina and the Great Smoky Mountains*, which included one of Elizabeth's paintings on the cover, and we were quite pleased when managing editor Kirsten Sutton asked us to undertake this anthology. We admire the level of professionalism The History Press staff always displays, and, in this instance, we are appreciative of the thorough editorial review provided by senior editor Hilary McCullough.

Our youngest daughter, Quintin Ellison, now a freelance writer and formerly an award-winning journalist with the *Asheville Citizen-Times*, critiqued each of the biographical essays. Our oldest daughter, M.L. Ellison-Murphree, provided computer assistance, proofread the bibliographical section and shared her research concerning Wilbur G. Zeigler and Ben S. Grosscup's *The Heart of the Alleghanies*.

1

THE JOURNEYS OF JAMES NEEDHAM
AND GABRIEL ARTHUR (1674)

Abraham Wood

Abraham Wood (circa 1615–circa 1681) was an indentured servant who arrived in Virginia in 1620. Having fulfilled his obligations, Wood moved in 1636 to what was then Virginia's southwestern frontier; that is, to the vicinity of the Appomattox River, where present Petersburg is located. He owned six hundred acres by 1639.

After Indians attacked Virginia's scattered Tidewater settlements in the mid-1640s, the colony's general assembly ordered the construction of four frontier forts. Fort Henry, built at the falls of the Appomattox River, was assigned to Wood, by then a captain in the militia. After a fall 1646 treaty transformed the Indians into tributaries, the general assembly appointed Wood proprietor of Fort Henry. Because the treaty designated his fort as one of only a few places where the Indians could legally trade, Wood had regular contact with tribes to the west and south. By the mid-1650s, he owned more than fifteen hundred acres and was a leading figure in negotiations and trade with the various tribes.

In a biographical sketch contributed to the *American National Biography Online* (2000), Virginia historian Alan Vance Briceland observed,

> *Wood's most significant contribution to the development of colonial America was as a participant in and organizer of English explorations of the Piedmont and the Appalachians. His goal, however, was not to open new lands so much as it was to discover an overland passage to the Pacific Ocean. Wood and others believed that the western ocean was just beyond the Appalachian Mountains. He informed an acquaintance that "I have been att ye charge to the value of two hundred pounds starling in ye discovery to ye south or west sea"…At his own expense, Wood dispatched Thomas Batts and Robert Fallam in September 1671 to attempt the first English crossing of the Appalachian Mountains. Their objective, set by Wood, was the discovery of "the ebbing and flowing of the [tidal] Waters on the other side of the Mountains." Entering the mountains by way of the New River Valley, Batts and Fallam traversed southern West Virginia to modern Matewan on the Kentucky border,*

a point some 185 miles west of Fort Henry. Wood's agents discovered that, while men could pass through the Appalachians, the route was too rugged to be developed for commerce…Two years later Wood dispatched James Needham and Gabriel Arthur to reconnoiter what the Indians spoke of as a more southerly passage "to the south or west sea." Accompanied by Indian guides, the exploring party entered the mountains near present Asheville, North Carolina, and emerged at modern Rome, Georgia. Arthur's account of his travels from Port Royal Sound to Mobile Bay, and from Florida's Apalachicola River to Kentucky's Big Sandy River, convinced Wood that the Pacific Ocean lay beyond reach. Although the Appalachians had been crossed twice, the western ocean had proved too distant and the obstacles to its discovery too numerous for Wood to finance continued explorations on his own…Wood's efforts had provided colonial Englishmen with their first realistic view of the dimensions and geography of the American Southeast.

Traveling from Virginia, Needham and Arthur arrived at Tomahitan, a Cherokee village situated near present Rome, Georgia, in early August 1763. After a few days of rest, Needham, accompanied by several Indian companions, headed to Virginia to report to Wood. Arthur stayed with the Tomahitan so as to learn their language and ensure the safe return of the Indians traveling with Needham. They arrived at Fort Henry on September 10. After debriefing Needham about the routes the men had followed and allowing him to rest for ten days, Wood sent him back to Tomahitan, along with his former companions and an Occaneeche Indian known to the English as Indian John. Along the trail, Needham and Indian John began feuding over the white man's treatment of one of the Tomahitan, who had "lett his pack slip into the water." A fight broke out between the two men at a camp on the west side of the Yadkin River. Indian John grabbed his musket and shot Needham dead.

Arthur remained with the Tomahitan and freely traveled with them on their raids and trading forays. According to Briceland, "In a year's time, Gabriel Arthur had traveled approximately 3,300 miles—2,500 on foot. He had perambulated the future states of Virginia, North Carolina, Georgia, South Carolina, Tennessee, Kentucky, and Alabama. He had laid eyes on, and may have also entered, portions of Florida and West Virginia. The breadth of his travels was incredibly wide for the seventeenth century. It would be a long time before another North American Englishman surpassed the range and extent of his travels." Aided by the chief of the Tomahitan, Arthur was allowed to return to Fort Henry on June 18, 1674, where he related his routes and exploits to Wood.

The only extant account of the travels of Needham and Arthur during 1673 and 1674 was provided by Wood in a letter dated August 22, 1674. It was addressed to his friend John Richards, treasurer for the Lords Proprietors of Carolina in London. This letter was subsequently filed with the Shaftesbury Papers in the Public Record Office, London, along with a memorandum endorsed by the famous philosopher John Locke, at that time secretary to the Earl of Shaftesbury.

Needham and Arthur's exact route over the Blue Ridge has been debated for more than a century. In his *Westward from Virginia: The Exploration of the Virginia-Carolina Frontier,*

In the Blue Ridge Mountains.

1650–1710 (1987), Briceland made a convincing argument—based on the topographical descriptions the explorers provided as well as the average mileage they would have traveled each day—that they traversed the valleys, rivers and gaps through Western North Carolina from present Morganton (where the Indian village of Sitteree was located) to present Asheville, and westward from there through what is now Canton and Waynesville. Passing over the Balsam Gap just west of Waynesville, they proceeded to present Sylva and Bryson City and over the gap at Topton to present Murphy "before passing into north Georgia just east of where the boundaries of North Carolina, Georgia, and Tennessee meet."

According to Briceland's calculations, the "five rivers" cited in Wood's letter that they would have had to ford in the Blue Ridge portion of their journey from Virginia to Georgia were the French Broad (at Asheville), the Pigeon (at Waynesville), the Tuckasegee (at Bryson City), the Little Tennessee (between Bryson City and Topton) and the Hiwassee (at Murphy). He noted that although there are two other rivers in the region—the Nantahala (west of Bryson City) and the Valley (east of Murphy)—they "did not have to be crossed by Needham and Arthur; they could be paralleled."

While crossing the Blue Ridge north of present Asheville in the early 1540s, Hernando de Soto's scribes entered some brief landscape descriptions in their journals. But in all likelihood, Abraham Wood's letter represents the first descriptions of the mountainous terrain of Western North Carolina penned in the English language. This selection is based on an edited modern language text of the letter.

To my Honoured Friend, Mr. Richards in London, present.

About the 10th of April, 1673, I sent out two Englishmen and eight Indians with accommodations for three months, but by misfortune and unwillingness of the Indians before the mountains that any should discover beyond them, my people returned affecting little, to be short. On the 17th of May, 1673, I sent them out again, with a like number of Indians and four horses. About the 25th of June they met with the Tomahittans as they were journeying from the mountains to the Occhonechees [a small but fierce tribe then situated on a major trading path at present Clarksville, Virginia]. *The Tomahittans told my men that, if an Englishman would stay with them, they would some of them come to my plantation with a letter which eleven of them did accordingly, and about forty of them promised to stay with my men at Occhonechee until the eleven returned. The effect of the letter was they resolved by God's Blessing to go through with the Tomahittans…*

    They journeyed nine days from Occhonechee to Sitteree, west and by south, past nine rivers and creeks which all end in this side the mountains and empty themselves into the east sea. Sitteree being the last town of inhabitance and not any path further until they came within two days' journey of the Tomahittans. They travel from thence up the mountains upon the sun setting all the way, and in four days get to the top, sometimes leading their horses sometimes riding. [They would have passed through either Hickorynut Gap or more probably Swannanoa Gap to access the plateau where Asheville is now situated.] *The ridge upon the top is not above two hundred paces over; the descent better than on this side. In half a day they came to the foot, and then level ground all the way, many slashes upon the heads of small runs. The slashes are full of very great canes and the water runs to the northwest. They pass five rivers* [in the Blue Ridge portion of North Carolina] *and about two hundred paces over the fifth being the middle most half a mile broad all sandy bottoms, with pebble stones, all fordable and all empty themselves northwest, when they travel upon the plains, from the mountains they go down, for several days they see straggly hills on their right hand, as they judge two days journey from them. By this time they have lost all their horses but one, not so much by the badness of the way as by hard travel, not having time to feed. When they lost sight of those hills they see a fog or smoke like a cloud from whence rain falls for several days on their right hand* [the Great Smoky Mountains] *as they travel still towards the sun setting great store of game, all along as turkeys, deer, elk, bear, wolf, and other vermin very tame. At the end of fifteen days from Sitteree they arrive at the Tomahittans river* [in the Georgia Piedmont], *being the sixth river from the mountains.*

Ab Wood
From Fort Henry, August the 22nd, 1674

2

THE SPANGENBERG DIARY (1752)

Bishop Augustus Gottlieb Spangenberg

In 1728, Colonel William Byrd of Virginia and his party completed a survey of the boundary line between Virginia and North Carolina from the Atlantic Ocean to Peters Creek in present Stokes County. From a high hill, they looked westward and saw the Blue Ridge front looming about thirty miles in the distance. Subsequently, Byrd lamented in his *History of the Dividing Line Run in the Year 1728*, "Our present circumstances wou'd not permit us to advance the Line to that Place, which the Hand of Nature had made so very remarkable."

Had Byrd and his party pushed on through the foothills of the Piedmont provinces of Virginia and North Carolina, they would have quickly penetrated the Blue Ridge. In that instance, given his abilities as a writer, any account Byrd might have fashioned would no doubt be regarded today as one of the high-water marks in the descriptive literature of Western North Carolina prior to the arrival of William Bartram in 1775. That honor, instead, must go to Bishop Augustus Gottlieb Spangenberg, who kept a fabulous diary in which he portrayed in considerable detail his exploration of the Blue Ridge in 1752 on behalf of the Moravian Church.

Spangenberg (1704–1792) was born in Prussia and in time became a professor of religion. He was acquainted with Count Nikolaus Ludwig von Zinzendorf and the Moravians and was much impressed with their missionary zeal. Indeed, his association with them gave such offense to his university colleagues that he was dismissed from his position. He responded by joining the Moravian Church and becoming Zinzendorf's assistant.

Spangenberg placed himself during the 1730s at the head of a body of Moravian immigrants and established a colony at Savannah, Georgia. By 1744 he had become overseer of the settlement at Bethlehem, Pennsylvania, where—with the exception of the period from 1749 to 1751, which he spent in Europe—he governed the church until 1761 with singular ability.

Spangenberg was dispatched to Edenton, North Carolina, in 1752. His assignment this time was to oversee the survey of a 100,000-acre tract of land in the North Carolina

Timber Wolves.

interior that John Carteret (Lord Granville) had offered to Zinzendorf. Starting out on September 10, 1752, the survey party traveled westward from the coast, headed for adventures that they could never have imagined.

By November 24, they had reached the foothills of the Blue Ridge in present Burke County, east of present Asheville. As Spangenberg noted in his diary, this was a land far beyond the meager comforts of the colonial frontier; his party had reached the true wilderness that then existed in the western portion of the Piedmont. Five days later they arrived at the foot of the Blue Ridge escarpment. The terrain they entered was so challenging that Spangenberg did not make another diary entry until December 5. By December 14, the Moravians had, after severe challenges, exited the Blue Ridge and returned to a camp in the Piedmont on the Yadkin River.

In October 1753, fifteen Moravians were chosen to leave Pennsylvania and journey to the backcountry in North Carolina that the Moravians had surveyed and now owned. They picked a surveyed tract called Wachau (later Wachovia) in the central Piedmont, where present Winston-Salem is now located. On Spangenberg's advice—based, after all, on firsthand experience—they chose to avoid settling in the western mountains or even near them. But the bishop's remarkable diary still contained the first detailed observations of the terrain, waterways, plants and animals of Western North Carolina.

(Notes by the editor of this anthology are in square brackets; those in pointed brackets appeared in the 1922 edition of *The Spangenberg Diary* edited by Adelaide L. Fries.)

Nov. 24th. From camp in the forks of the third river <Upper Creek Burke County, sometimes called Warrior Fork> *that flows into the Catawba near Quaker Meadows. Perhaps five miles from Table Mountain. This is the fifth tract that we have selected, and contains seven or eight hundred acres—a fine piece of land, lying on two creeks…The land is very rich, and has been much frequented by buffalo, whose tracks are everywhere, and can often be followed with profit. Frequently, however, a man cannot travel them, for they go through thick and thin, through morass and deep water, and up and down banks so steep that a man could fall down but neither ride nor walk! The wolves here give us music every morning, from six corners at once, such music as I have never heard. They are not like the wolves of Germany, Poland, and Livonia, but are afraid of men, and do not usually approach near them. A couple of Brethren skilled in hunting would be of benefit not only here but at our other tracts, partly to kill the wolves and panthers, partly to supply the Brethren with game. Not only can the skins of wolves and panthers be sold, but the government pays a bounty of ten shillings for each one killed.*

Nov. 28. Old Indian Field, on the north-east branch <Mulberry Creek, Caldwell County> *of Middle Little River. We reached here on the 25th of this month, camped beside the branch, looked over the land, and resolved to take it up. It is lowland, lying on two streams, the one somewhat larger, the other somewhat smaller than our Manocasy at Bethlehem. The water that we find in these mountains is excellent, better than the spring at Bethlehem. It looks as though there might be mineral springs about. The streams on this tract afford good mill sites, and apparently will neither go dry in summer nor freeze in winter, for they are fresh spring water. There are more than twenty springs on this tract, with little runs, beside which canes grow freely…*

Nov. 29. From the camp in the upper fork <Wilson's Creek, a branch of Johns River> *of the Second or Middle Little River, flowing into the Catawba, not far from Quaker Meadows. We are here in a region that has perhaps been seldom visited since the creation of the world. We are some 70 or 80 miles from the last settlement in North Carolina, and have come over terrible mountains, and often through very dangerous ways. But, thank God, we are all well, cheerful, and content, and thankful to our Heavenly Father for His gracious protection and care, to our dear Lord for His presence and friendship, to the Holy Spirit for His unwearied workings, and to the Holy Angels for the guidance of which we have had many marked evidences. From here we plan to go to the heads of the Atkin* <Yadkin River>, *a large river, but on account of its terrible falls and numerous rocks useless for commerce. Now concerning the place where we are now in camp. It is a depression, a "little Oli"* <meaning "a hole" in the Indian language>, *the richest we have yet seen in North Carolina. Three streams flow through it, and there are many sweet springs. There is an abundance of wood. Our horses find plenty of tender grass in the feeding ground of the buffalo, and around the springs, and they eat eagerly…*

Dec. 5th, from camp in an Indian field, on what we think is a south branch of the Atkin. We have reached here after a hard journey over very high, terrible, mountains and cliffs. A hunter, whom we had taken to show us the way, and who once knew the path to the Atkin, missed the trail, and led us into a place from where there was no way out except by climbing an indescribably steep mountain. Part of the way we climbed on hands and knees, dragging after us the loads we had taken from the backs of the horses, for had we not unsaddled them they would have fallen backwards down the mountain—indeed, this did happen once; part of the way we led the horses, who were trembling like a leaf. When we reached the top we saw mountains to right and to left, before and behind us, many hundreds of mountains, rising like great waves in a storm. <It is evident that they missed what is now known as Mulberry Gap between the head of Mulberry Creek and the Yadkin, and instead followed the main branch of Johns River up through the "Globe" to its head at Blowing Rock, Watauga County.> *We rested a little, and then began to descend, not quite so precipitately. Soon we found water, and oh, how refreshing it was! Then we sought pasturage for our horses, riding a long way, and well into the night, but found nothing except dry leaves. We could have wept for pity for the poor beasts. It had become so dark that we could not put up the tent, and were obliged to camp under the trees. It was a trying night! In the morning we went further, but had to cut our way through laurel bushes and beaver dams, which greatly wearied our company. We changed our course, and leaving the ravine went up on the mountain, and there in a chestnut grove the Lord showed us a good spring, and forage for our horses. He also sent us two deer in our necessity, which were most welcome. Next day we went on, and came to a creek, so full of rocks that we could not follow it, and with banks so steep that a horse could not climb them, and scarcely a man. We ate a little, but our horses had nothing, absolutely nothing, and that distressed us. Presently one of our hunters, who had been up on the mountain, returned with the report that he had seen a meadow, so we cut our way through the bushes to it, reaching it by evening, to the delight of men and horses.* <This tract included the site of the present town of Boone, Watauga County.> *We put up our tent, but had barely finished when there came such a wind storm that we could hardly stand against it. I think I have never felt a winter wind so strong and so cold. The ground was covered with snow; water froze beside the fire. Then our men lost heart! What should we do? Our horses would die, and we with them. For the hunters had about concluded that we were across the crest of the Blue Mountains, and on the Mississippi watershed. The next day the sun came out, and the days were warmer, though the nights still very cold. Br. Antes and I rode over the tract, and think that it contains about 5000 acres. Much of it is already clear, long grass grows here, and it is all low-land. Three creeks unite in a river that flows into the Ohio, and with the Ohio into the Mississippi…*

Dec. 14th. From the camp on Atkin Waters, where a north and a south branch unite, forming the river which flows through North and South Carolina. [The Spangenberg party had retreated from the Blue Ridge and was camped once again on the Yadkin River.] *Here we are at last, after a difficult journey among the mountains. We were completely lost, and whichever way we turned we were walled in. Not one of our company had ever been there before, and path or trail were unknown—though how can one speak of path or trail when none existed? We crossed only dry mountains and dry valleys, and when for several days we followed the river* <New River> *in the hope that it would lead us out we found ourselves only deeper in the wilderness, for the river ran now north, now south, now east, now west, in short to all points of the compass! Finally we decided to leave the river and take a course between east and south, crossing the mountains as best we could. One height rose behind the other, and we traveled between hope and fear, distressed for our horses, which had nothing to eat. At last we reached a stream* [the Lewis Fork of the Yadkin River, about twenty miles northeast of Blowing Rock] *flowing rapidly down the mountain, followed it, and happily reached this side of the Blue Ridge. We also found pasturage for our horses, and oh, how glad we were!*

3

THE HISTORY OF THE AMERICAN INDIANS (1775)

James Adair

Trader and author James Adair (1709–circa 1787) was born in County Antrim, Ireland. He moved to South Carolina in 1735 and immediately began trading with the Overhill Cherokee, whose towns were beyond the Great Smoky Mountains along the lower Little Tennessee River in present east Tennessee. By the early 1840s, he was trading with the Catawba in the Piedmont region of North and South Carolina. From there, he moved west to present north Mississippi to trade with the Chickasaw. The "cheerful, brave Chikkasah" were always Adair's favorites among the Indian tribes.

During the 1760s, Adair wrote a history of the Indians among whom he had lived for decades. He voyaged to England in 1775 to get his book published. It appeared that year with the marvelously descriptive title page:

> *The HISTORY of the AMERICAN INDIANS, Particularly Those Nations Adjoining to the Mississippi, East and West Florida, Georgia, South and North Carolina. Containing an Account of Their Origin, Language, Manners, Religious and Civil Customs, Laws, Form of Government, Punishments, Conduct in War and Domestic Life, Their Habits, Diet, Agriculture, Manufactures, Diseases and Method of Cure, and Other Particulars, Sufficient to Render it A COMPLETE INDIAN SYSTEM, with Observations on Former Historians, the Conduct of Our Colony, Governors, Superintendents, Missionaries, &C. Also AN APPENDIX Containing a Description of the Floridas and the Mississippi Lands, with Their Productions; the Benefits of Colonizing Georgiana and Civilizing the Indians; and the Way to Make All the Colonies More Valuable to the Mother Country. With a New Map of the Country Referred to in the History. By James Adair, Esquire, a Trader with the Indians, and Resident in Their Country for Forty Years. London: Printed for Edward and Charles Dilly, in the Poultry. MDCCLXXV.*

According to recent scholarship, Adair's book is not always reliable as a history of his own time. But his firsthand descriptions of southeastern Indian cultures are still

Uktena.

accepted, despite the author's obsessive arguments that the lost tribes of Israel were ancestors of American Indians.

In her annotated edition of Adair's book published by the University of Alabama Press in 2005, editor and historian Kathryn E. Holland Braund noted,

> *Today historians, ethnohistorians and anthropologists regard Adair's* History of the American Indians *as one of the most valuable primary accounts of the southeastern Indians…Adair's long tenure among the southern tribes as a deerskin trader presented many opportunities for intimate observation of Indian culture, and his broad education and literary skill provided him with the tools to build an incredibly detailed and singular account of life among the eighteenth-century southern Indians.*

Adair devoted a full chapter titled "Account of the Cheerake Nation, &c." to his observations regarding Cherokee landscapes, lifestyles and lore. In that chapter, he described giant supernatural rattlesnakes the Indians referred to as "chieftains of the snakes." According to the Cherokee belief system, the cosmos was divided into three realms. The Upper World of light, peace and the hereafter was symbolized by giant mythic hawks called Sanuwas. The Middle World was the everyday mundane realm in which humans resided. The Under World of darkness, decay and death was symbolized by giant serpents called Uktenas. These serpents were reported to have quartz crystals in their foreheads that flashed like beacon lights, attracting humans to their certain demise. The serpents Adair described had the crystals (carbuncles), but not the set of antlers the Cherokees also usually associated with Uktenas.

> [The national name of the Cherokees] *is derived from Chee-ra, "fire," which is their reputed lower heaven, and hence they call their magi, Cheera'-tahge, "men possessed of the divine fire." The country lies in about 34 degrees north latitude, at the distance of 340 computed miles to the north-west of Charlestown—140 miles west-south-west from the Katahba nation—and almost 200 miles to the north of the Muskohge or Creek country…*
>
> *Their towns are always close to some river, or creek; as there the land is commonly very level and fertile, on account of the frequent washings off the mountains, and the moisture it receives from the waters, that run through their fields. And such a situation enables them to perform the ablutions, connected with their religious worship.*
>
> *The eastern, or lower parts of this country, are sharp and cold to a Carolinian in winter, and yet agreeable: but those towns that lie among the Apalahche mountains, are very pinching to such who are unaccustomed to a savage life. The ice and snow continue on the north-side, till late in the spring of the year: however, the natives are well provided for it, by their bathing and anointing themselves. This regimen shuts up the pores of the body, and by that means prevents too great a perspiration; and an accustomed exercise of hunting, joined with the former, puts them far above their climate: they are almost as impenetrable to cold, as a bar of steel, and the severest cold is no detriment to their hunting…*

Their towns are still scattered wide of each other, because the land will not admit any other settlement: it is a rare thing to see a level tract of four hundred acres. They are also strongly attached to rivers—all retaining the opinion of the ancients, that rivers are necessary to constitute a paradise. Nor is it only ornamental, but likewise beneficial to them, on account of purifying themselves, and also for the services of common life— such as fishing, fowling, and killing of deer, which come in the warm season, to eat the saltish moss and grass, which grow on the rocks, and under the surface of the waters. Their rivers are generally very shallow, and pleasant to the eye; for the land being high, the waters have a quick descent; they seldom overflow their banks, unless when a heavy rain falls on a deep snow. Then, it is frightful to see the huge pieces of ice, mixed with a prodigious torrent of water, rolling down the high mountains, and over the steep craggy rocks, so impetuous, that nothing can resist their force…

In the lower and middle parts of this mountainous ragged country, the Indians have a convenient passable path, by the foot of the mountains: but farther in, they are of such a prodigious height, that they are forced to wind from north to south, along the rivers and large creeks, to get a safe passage: and the paths are so steep in many places, that the horses often pitch, and rear on end, to scramble up. Several of the mountains are some miles from bottom to top, according to the ascent of the paths: and there are other mountains I have seen from these, when out with the Indians in clear weather, that the eye can but faintly discern, which therefore must be at a surprising distance…

From the head of the southern branch of Savanah-river, it does not exceed half a mile to a head spring of the Missisippi-water, that runs through the middle and upper parts of the Cheerake nation, about a north-west course—and joining other rivers, they empty themselves into the great Missisippi. The above fountain, is called "Herbert's spring" and it was natural for strangers to drink thereof, to quench thirst, gratify their curiosity, and have it to say they had drank of the French waters. Some of our people, who went only with the view of staying a short time, but by some allurement or other, exceeded the time appointed, at their return, reported either through merriment or superstition, that the spring had such a natural bewitching quality, that whosoever drank of it, could not possibly quit the nation, during the tedious space of seven years…

Although the Cheerake shewed such little skill in curing the small pox, yet they, as well as all other Indian nations, have a great knowledge of specific virtues in simples; applying herbs and plants, on the most dangerous occasions, and seldom if ever, fail to effect a thorough cure, from the natural bush. In the order of nature, every country and climate is blest with specific remedies for the maladies that are connatural to it—naturalists tell us they have observed, that when the wild goat's sight begins to decay, he rubs his head against a thorn, and by some effluvia, or virtue in the vegetable, the sight is renewed. Thus the snake recovers after biting any creature, by his knowledge of the proper antidote; and many of our arts and forms of living, are imitated by lower ranks of the animal creation: the Indians, instigated by nature, and quickened by experience, have discovered the peculiar properties of vegetables, as far as needful in their situation of life. For my own part, I would prefer an old Indian before any chirurgeon [surgeon] whatsoever, in curing green wounds by bullets, arrows, &c. both for the certainty, ease, and speediness of cure; for if those parts of the body are not hurt, which are essential to the preservation of life, they cure the wounded in a trice. They bring the patient into a good temperament of body, by a decoction of proper herbs and roots, and always enjoin a most abstemious life: they forbid them women, salt, and every kind of flesh-meat, applying mountain alum [alumroot, *Heuchera americana*, an antiseptic], as the chief ingredient…

I do not remember to have seen or heard of an Indian dying by the bite of a snake, when out at war, or a hunting; although they are then often bitten by the most dangerous snakes—every one carries in his shot-pouch, a piece of the best snake-root, such as the Seneeka [Seneca snakeroot, *Polygala senega*], or fern-snake-root [rattlesnake grape fern, *Botrychium virginianum*], or the wild hore-hound, wild plantain, St. Andrew's cross, and a variety of other herbs and roots, which are plenty, and well known to those who range the American woods, and are exposed to such dangers, and will effect a thorough and speedy cure if timely applied. When an Indian perceives he is struck by a snake, he immediately chews some of the root, and having swallowed a sufficient quantity of it, he applies some to the wound; which he repeats as occasion requires, and in proportion to the poison the snake has infused into the wound. For a short space of time, there is a terrible conflict through all the body, by the jarring qualities of the burning poison, and the strong antidote; but the poison is soon repelled through the same channels it entered, and the patient is cured…

Between the heads of the northern branch [Little Tennessee] of the lower Cheerake river, and the heads of that of Tuckasehchee [Tuckasegee], winding round in a long course by the late Fort-Loudon, and afterwards into the Missisippi, there is, both in the nature and circumstances, a great phaenomenon. Between two high mountains, nearly covered with old mossy rocks, lofty cedars, and pines, in the valleys of which the beams of the sun reflect a powerful heat, there are, as the natives affirm, some bright old inhabitants, or rattle snakes, of a more enormous size than is mentioned in history. They are so large and unwieldy, that they take a circle, almost as wide as their length, to crawl round in their shortest orbit: but bountiful nature compensates the heavy motion of their bodies, for as they say, no living creature moves within the reach of their sight, but they can draw it to them; which is agreeable to what we observe, through the whole system of animated beings. Nature endues them with proper capacities to sustain life—as they cannot support themselves, by their speed, or cunning to spring from an ambuscade, it is needful they should have the bewitching craft of their eyes and forked tongues.

The description the Indians give us of their colour, is as various as what we are told of the camelion, that seems to the spectator to change its colour, by every different position he may view it in; which proceeds from the piercing rays of light that blaze from their foreheads, so as to dazzle the eyes, from whatever quarter they post themselves—for in each of their heads, there is a large carbuncle [quartz crystal], which not only repels, but they affirm, sullies the meridian beams of the sun. They reckon it so dangerous to disturb those creatures, that no temptation can induce them to betray their secret recess to the prophane. They call them and all of the rattle-snake *kind, kings, or chieftains of the snakes; and they allow one such to every different species of the brute creation. An old trader of Cheeowhee told me, that for the reward of two pieces of stroud-cloth, he engaged a couple of young warriors to shew him the place of their resort; but the head-men would not by any means allow it, on account of a superstitious tradition—for they fancy the killing of them would expose them to the danger of being bit by the other inferior species of that serpentine tribe, who love their chieftains, and know by instinct those who maliciously killed them, as they fight only in their own defence, and that of their young ones, never biting those who do not disturb them. Although they esteem those rattle snakes as chieftains of that species, yet they do not deify them, as the Egyptians did all the serpentine kind, and likewise ibis, that preyed upon them; however, it seems to have sprung from the same origin, for I once saw the Chikkasah Archimagus to chew some snake-root, blow it on his hands, and then take up a rattle snake without damage—soon afterwards he laid it down carefully, in a hollow tree, lest I should have killed it.*

4.
BARTRAM'S TRAVELS (1791)

William Bartram

Artist, naturalist, explorer and author William Bartram (1739–1823) was born in Philadelphia, Pennsylvania. Bartram has become the patron saint of American naturalists. With his ability to combine intimate personal experience with genuine scientific observation, this country—indeed the world—had seen nothing like him. He was an American original whose influence on his contemporaries was enormous and continues to this day.

As a youth, Bartram displayed a talent for drawing specimens collected by his father, John Bartram, America's first botanist. But he initially worked as a merchant and trader. In 1765, he accompanied his father on an expedition to Florida and decided to remain in the American South, drawing the flora, gathering botanical specimens, becoming an accomplished ornithologist and befriending both colonial planters and members of indigenous tribes. Between 1773 and 1777, he made his famous journey throughout what was to become the Southeastern portion of the United States. The riveting summary of his observations and adventures appeared in 1791 as *Travels Through North & South Carolina, Georgia, East & West Florida, the Cherokee Country, the Extensive Territories of the Muscogulges, or Creek Confederacy, and the Country of the Chactaws; Containing An Account of the Soil and Natural Productions of Those Regions, Together with Observations on the Manners of the Indians.*

Bartram's Travels—as the volume is generally known—quickly became an American classic, being described by one modern scholar as "the most astounding verbal artifact of the early republic." The book was also an enormous success in Europe, where it had a great influence upon two towering poets of the budding Romantic movement. Samuel Taylor Coleridge practically memorized it. His notebooks were filled with excerpts, and his poem "Kubla Khan" echoed phrases lifted almost intact from Bartram's text. William Wordsworth carried a copy with him to Germany, where, having lost it, he wrote home insisting that another be sent immediately. Cooper, Thoreau, Emerson and Chateaubriand all borrowed inspiration and imagery from the wandering naturalist's account of his solitary travels, as have numerous modern writers.

Rosebay Rhododendron.

Bartram was only in Western North Carolina for a short while during the late spring of 1775. His route was up the Indian Path from Charleston, South Carolina, through present Clayton, Georgia, and along the Little Tennessee River to present Franklin, where he described the Nikwasi mound and community site. From there, Bartram continued down the Little Tennessee to the important Cowee mound and village site, where the varied observations and encounters in this selection were recorded.

> *I travelled about five miles through old plantations, now under grass, but appeared to have been planted the last season; the soil exceeding fertile, loose, black, deep and fat. I arrived at Cowe [Cowee] about noon; this settlement is esteemed the capital town; it is situated on the bases of the hills on both sides of the river, near to its bank, and here terminates the great vale of Cowe, exhibiting one of the most charming natural mountainous landscapes perhaps any where to be seen; ridges of hills rising grand and sublimely one above and beyond another, some boldly and majestically advancing into the verdant plain, their feet bathed with the silver flood of the Tanase [Little Tennessee] whilst others far distant, veiled in blue mists, sublimely mount aloft, with yet greater majesty lift up their pompous crests and overlook vast regions.*

The vale is closed at Cowe by a ridge of mighty hills, called the Jore mountain [Nantahala Mountains], *said to be the highest land in the Cherokee country, which crosses the Tanase here.*

On my arrival at this town I waited on the gentlemen to whom I was recommended by letter, and was received with respect and every demonstration of hospitality and friendship.

I took my residence with Mr. Galahan the chief trader here, an ancient respectable man who had been many years a trader in this country, and is esteemed and beloved by the Indians for his humanity, probity and equitable dealings with them…

Next day after my arrival I crossed the river in a canoe, on a visit to a trader who resided amongst the habitations on the other shore. After dinner, on his mentioning some curious scenes amongst the hills, some miles distance from the river, we agreed to spend the afternoon in observations on the mountains.

After riding near two miles through Indian plantations of Corn, which was well cultivated, kept clean of weeds and was well advanced, being near eighteen inches in height, and the Beans planted at the Corn hills were above ground; we leave the fields on our right, turning towards the mountains and ascending through a delightful green vale or lawn, which conducted us in amongst the pyramidal hills and crossing a brisk flowing creek, meandering through the meads which continued near two miles, dividing and branching in amongst the hills; we then mounted their steep ascents, rising gradually by ridges or steps one above another, frequently crossing narrow, fertile dales as we ascended; the air feels cool and animating, being charged with the fragrant breath of the mountain beauties, the blooming mountain cluster Rose, blushing Rhododendron and fair Lilly of the valley: having now attained the summit of this very elevated ridge, we enjoyed a fine prospect indeed; the enchanting Vale of Keowe, perhaps as celebrated for fertility, fruitfulness and beautiful prospects as the Fields of Pharsalia or the Vale of Tempe: the town, the elevated peeks of the Jore mountains, a very distant prospect of the Jore village in a beautiful lawn, lifted up many thousand feet higher than our present situation, besides a view of many other villages and settlements on the sides of the mountains, at various distances and elevations; the silver rivulets gliding by them and snow white cataracts glimmering on the sides of the lofty hills; the bold promontories of the Jore mountain stepping into the Tanase river, whilst his foaming waters rushed between them. [Bartram probably made these panoramic observations from the general area of Cowee Bald, situated near where present Jackson, Macon and Swain Counties corner in the Cowee Mountains at 5,085 feet. From that vantage point, he would have been looking westward back over the Little Tennessee River Valley into the Nantahalas.]

After viewing this very entertaining scene we began to descend the mountain on the other side, which exhibited the same order of gradations of ridges and vales as on our ascent, and at length rested on a very expansive, fertile plain, amidst the towering hills, over which we rode a long time, through magnificent high forests, extensive green fields, meadows and lawns. Here had formerly been a very flourishing settlement, but the Indians deserted it in search of fresh planting land, which they soon found in a rich vale but a few miles distance over a ridge of hills. Soon after entering on these charming, sequestered, prolific fields, we came to a fine little river, which crossing, and riding over fruitful strawberry beds and green lawns, on the sides of a circular ridge of hills in front of us, and going round the bases of this promontory, came to a fine meadow on an arm of the vale, through which meandered a brook, its humid vapours bedewing the fragrant strawberries which hung in heavy red clusters over the grassy verge; we crossed the rivulet, then rising a sloping, green, turfy ascent, alighted on the borders of a grand forest of stately trees, which we penetrated on foot a little distance to a horse-stamp, where was a large squadron of those useful creatures, belonging to my friend and companion, the trader, on the sight of whom they assembled together from all quarters; some at a distance saluted him with shrill neighings of gratitude, or came prancing up to lick the salt out of his hand; whilst the younger and more timorous came galloping onward, but coyly wheeled off, and fetching a circuit stood aloof, but as soon as their lord and master strewed the chrystaline salty bait on the hard beaten ground, they all, old and young, docile and timorous, soon formed themselves in ranks and fell to licking up the delicious morsel.

It was a fine sight; more beautiful creatures I never saw; there were of them of all colours, sizes and dispositions. Every year as they become of age he sends off a troop of them down to Charleston, where they are sold to the highest bidder.

Having paid our attention to this useful part of the creation, who, if they are under our dominion, have consequently a right to our protection and favour. We returned to our trusty servants that were regaling themselves in the exuberant sweet pastures and strawberry fields in sight, and mounted again; proceeding on our return to town, continued through part of this high forest skirting on the meadows; began to ascend the hills of a ridge which we were under the necessity of crossing, and having gained its summit, enjoyed a most enchanting view, a vast expanse of green meadows and strawberry fields; a meandering river gliding through, saluting in its various turnings the swelling, green, turfy knolls, embellished with parterres of flowers and fruitful strawberry beds; flocks of turkies strolling about them; herds of deer prancing in the meads or bounding over the hills; companies of young, innocent Cherokee virgins, some busily gathering the rich fragrant fruit, others having already filled their baskets, lay reclined under the shade of floriferous and fragrant native bowers of Magnolia, Azalea, Philadelphus [syringa]*, perfumed Calycanthus* [sweet shrub], *sweet Yellow Jessamine and cerulian Glycine frutescens* [possibly ground nut, *Apios americana*] *disclosing their beauties to the fluttering breeze, and bathing their limbs in the cool fleeting streams; whilst other parties, more gay and libertine, were yet Collecting strawberries or wantonly chasing their companions, tantalising them, staining their lips and cheeks with the rich fruit.*

This sylvan scene of primitive innocence was enchanting, and perhaps too enticing for hearty young men long to continue idle spectators.

In fine, nature prevailing over reason, we wished at least to have a more active part in their delicious sports. Thus precipitately resolving, we cautiously made our approaches, yet undiscovered, almost to the joyous scene of action. Now, although we meant no other than an innocent frolic with this gay assembly of hamadryades, we shall leave it to the person of feeling and sensibility to form an idea to what lengths our passions might have hurried us, thus warmed and excited, had it not been for the vigilance and care of some envious matrons who lay in ambush, and espying us gave the alarm, time enough for the nymphs to rally and assemble together; we however pursued and gained ground on a group of them, who had incautiously strolled to a greater distance from their guardians, and finding their retreat now like to be cut off, took shelter under cover of a little grove, but on perceiving themselves to be discovered by us, kept their station, peeping through the bushes; when observing our approaches, they confidently discovered themselves and decently advanced to meet us, half unveiling their blooming faces, incarnated with the modest maiden blush, and with native innocence and cheerfulness presented their little baskets, merrily telling us their fruit was ripe and sound.

We accepted a basket, sat down and regaled ourselves on the delicious fruit, encircled by the whole assembly of the innocently jocose sylvan nymphs; by this time the several parties under the conduct of the elder matrons, had disposed themselves in companies on the green, turfy banks.

My young companion, the trader, by concessions and suitable apologies for the bold intrusion, having compromised the matter with them, engaged them to bring their collections to his house at a stipulated price, we parted friendly.

And now taking leave of these Elysian fields, we again mounted the hills, which we crossed, and traversing obliquely their flowery beds, arrived in town in the cool of the evening.

5

PORTIONS OF THE JOURNAL OF ANDRÉ MICHAUX, BOTANIST, WRITTEN DURING HIS TRAVELS IN THE UNITED STATES AND CANADA, 1785–1796

André Michaux

Botanist André Michaux (1746–1802) was born at Satory, the royal estate adjacent to Versailles, France, where his father, also named André Michaux, was employed as overseer. His father, who tutored the boy in regard to both horticulture and botany, died by the time Michaux was twenty years old. In that instance, he and his younger brother jointly managed the Satory estate.

In 1779, Michaux moved to Paris and lived near the Jardin du Roi (Jardin des Plantes after the Revolution), where he met André Thouin, the chief gardener and a skilled naturalizer of plants. Two years later, Michaux received a commission to undertake a trip to Persia, from which he sent back seeds and specimens to France. On his return in 1785 he brought back rich plant and natural history collections.

Concerned about the dwindling supply of good timber for the country's navy, the French government, in 1785, commissioned Michaux to visit North America in search of suitable trees that could be cultivated in France. He traveled with his young son, Francois André Michaux, who would eventually rival his father as an explorer and collector of plants.

Michaux had been expressly instructed to set up a nursery from which seeds and seedlings could be shipped to France. He acquired land for that purpose in 1786 near Hackensack, New Jersey. On a visit to Philadelphia, he met William Bartram—who was busy writing his famous *Travels*, which would be published in 1791—and visited his garden. It's probable that they discussed the wealth of plant materials Bartram had observed in 1775, during his brief sojourn in the Carolina mountains.

Michaux went south the following year with his son and established a second nursery at Charleston, South Carolina. From that home base, they explored the southern Appalachians for the first time. Toward the end of 1788, they again explored the area of present Oconee County, South Carolina, where Michaux made the first collection of the elusive *Shortia* (see below). In 1879, on their way to Philadelphia, the father and son team visited the mountains of Carolina.

Shortia.

In 1792, Michaux conferred with Thomas Jefferson about making an expedition to the west by way of the Missouri River, with funding raised by the American Philosophical Society. But before Michaux could leave, Edmond-Charles Genet, the new French minister in America, arrived in Charleston and preempted the trip. It was an expedition that would be successfully accomplished just over a decade later by Meriwether Lewis and William Clark.

Michaux made an additional trip to the Carolina mountains in 1794. In the following year, he ventured as far as the Mississippi River, returning in April 1796 for the last time to Charleston. Since he had exhausted his own finances and had not received any money from the French government for some time, he decided to abandon his explorations and return to France. Michaux described nearly one thousand species of North American plants. He also introduced a large number of American trees into France and introduced other trees into North America, including crape myrtle, chinaberry and ginko.

In *The Appalachians* (1965), eminent naturalist Maurice Brooks observed, "*Shortia* should probably stand as the archetype of Appalachian plants." No other native southern Appalachian wildflower has been more sought after or treasured—and there might not be a prettier wildflower in the world. *Shortia galacifolia*, which bears the common names *Shortia* and Oconee bells, is native to seven restricted locations in the mountains and foothills of Georgia, North Carolina and South Carolina. As previously noted, it was first collected in its fruiting stage by Michaux in 1788. He deposited a single specimen in the herbarium of the Jardin des Plantes, with the cryptic notation that it had been found in "les haunts montagnes de Carolinie."

In 1839, Asa Gray—America's first great academic botanist—discovered Michaux's specimen in Paris and named it in honor of Charles W. Short, a professor at the University of Kentucky. Wanting to see the plant in bloom in its native setting, Gray led an expedition in 1841 into the "high mountains" of North Carolina a hundred miles or so north of where Michaux had made his collections. For decades thereafter, the frustrated Harvard professor cajoled numerous botanists and plant hunters into searching for his "lost plant."

In 1877, a small stand of *Shortia* was discovered near Marion in McDowell County, about seventy miles northwest of Michaux's collection site. Then, in the fall of 1886, that site was finally rediscovered by a team of plant hunters led by botanist C.S. Sargent, one of Gray's students, who became the first director of the Arnold Arboretum. A member of Sargent's team returned the following spring and found the plant in full bloom: "Masses of dainty little white, fringed bells, each swaying in the mountain breeze on its pink-tinted stem, rising about six inches from a rosette of glossy scalloped leaves." According to Michaux's biographers, Henry and Elizabeth Savage, "A box of the then flowering *Shortia* was sent to Dr. Gray. It is said that the old botanist, then in his seventy-eighth year, wept with joy."

In 1889, selections from Michaux's journals were edited by Sargent, with expository notes, and published in the *Proceedings of the American Philosophical Society* as "Portions of the Journal of André Michaux, Botanist, Written During His Travels in the United States and Canada, 1785–1796." Michaux's journal entries—which one observer described as "crudely laconic"—have received scant literary attention. But they are of considerable interest to those concerned with the natural history of the southern Appalachians. The following brief selection includes the description of his discovery of *Shortia* in the northwestern corner of South Carolina as well as several examples of his journal entries made during collecting trips in the mountains of Western North Carolina.

On December 8, 1788, as we were approaching the source of the Kiwi [Keowee River] *the paths became more difficult…In this area there was a small hut inhabited by a family of Cherokee Indians. We stopped there to camp and I rushed to do some exploring. I gathered a new low plant* [Shortia galacifolia] *with saw-toothed leaves spreading over a hill a short distance from the river…*

On the eleventh of December there was a hard frost and the air turned clear and very crisp. With my guides, I returned to the head of the Kiwi…and I collected a large amount of that plant with the saw-toothed leaves that I had found the first day of my arrival. I did not encounter it on any other mountains. The Indians here say the leaves taste well when chewed and that their smell was good when they were crumpled, which I found to be true. [Michaux then entered in his journal the "Directions for Finding the Plants" that C.S. Sargent used to relocate the type locality in 1886.]

November 24, 1789 crossed the Blue Ridges in N. Carolina. The 25th arrived at the lower region of the Black Mountain and collected Azalea fluva [flame azalea, *Rhododendron calendulaceum*], *Azalea nova* [?] *species, &c.*

December 1*st* through the 5*th* of the same visited several high Mountains and then packed up my Harvest in the quantity of 2500 trees, Bushes and plants, in all 7 crates.

The 31*st* [July 1794] collected on the Lineville [Linville] high mountains to the South-East of Ainsworth's house and on Rocks and the mountains devoid of trees a small shrub Clethra buxifolia [sweet pepperbush, Clethra acuminata].

6

STROTHER'S SURVEY DIARY (1799)

John Strother

O ne of the more interesting early accounts of the topography, flora, fauna and other aspects of Western North Carolina is contained in a diary kept by John Strother (?–1815), who in 1799 was appointed one of the surveyors charged with delineating a portion of the boundary between Tennessee and North Carolina. Strother was born in Culpepper County, Virginia. He traveled in the mid-1780s to Georgia, where he became involved in a plan to secure a large tract of land at Muscle Shoals in the bend of the Tennessee River. When that didn't work out, he moved to southeastern North Carolina. By 1795, he was surveying and mapping more than 850,000 acres owned by John Gray Blount. He subsequently surveyed and mapped other holdings throughout the Piedmont region of the state and in the Blue Ridge. He is believed to have been living in Asheville at the time of his death.

Of particular interest in these excerpts from Strother's diary are his descriptions of an encounter with a large rattlesnake (which he described as a "rattlebug"), the extensive grassy balds at Roan Mountain and the "pictures" he claimed to have seen at "Painted Rock" (Paint Rock) in 1790 that were no longer visible in 1799. The name of the settlement on the French Broad River then known as Warm Springs was changed to Hot Springs in 1886.

May 12th, 1799—Set out from Asheville, Buncombe County, in order to meet ye commissioners appointed by the State of North Carolina to run the line between the state & ye state of Tennessee. At Capt. Robt. Nalls on New River where I arrived the 17th instant, met with Major Mussendine Matthews, one of the Commissioners, his son & Mr. Robt. Logan, chain bearers & markers waiting the arrival of Genl. Joseph McDowell & Col. David Vance, the other two commissioners & the rest of the company.

Ye 18th—No news of McDowell & Vance. Went to Mr. Elsburg's to wait their arrival.

Timber Rattlesnake.

19ᵗʰ—Still at Elsburgs in a state of suspense.

*20ᵗʰ—Col. Vance and Major B. Collins arrived last night. We left Elsburg's &
went to Capt. Issac Weaver's where the company all met, composed of the following
gentlemen (to wit) Genl. Jos. McDowell, Col. D. Vance, Major Mussendine
Matthews, commissioners. Myself & Mr. Robt. Henry, surveyors; Messers B. Collins,
James Hawkins, George Penland, Robt Logan, Geo. Davidson & Josiah Matthews,
chain bearers and markers; Major James Neely, commissary; two pack horse men & a
pilot. Set out from Weavers went half a mile and camped on Stag Creek…*

*22ⁿᵈ—After taking a hearty breakfast we set out & ascended the Stone Mountain to
ye top; found it very steep & the name very applicable. Continued on the mountain
3/4 mile to a place called the Upper Rye Patch where we encamped and Major
Matthews, myself, the pilot & two chain bearers set out in order to find the place where*

the Virginia Line crossed the extreme height of the Stone Mountain. After some hours search we found it in a low Gap between the head of Horsepen Creek of New River & a branch of Laurell of Holston River, 2 or 3 miles SW from the Whitetop Mountain. We run the line between the State of N.C. & T. on the extreme height of the Stone Mn to our camp at the upper Rye Patch, where we feasted sumptuously on stewed venison & bacon while the rest of the company went back to see the place where we set out with the line from ye Virginia…

25th—We had a very disagreeable night the morning appears gloomy—some of our horses lost. Mr. Logan cut his foot; it will be bad. The horses were at length found. We all eat our breakfast & set out on the line, went 3/4 mile. It set in and rained hard and obliged us to take up camp at the first place that offered, which was a branch of Roan's Creek, where we spent an uncomfortable evening. The next day being the Lard's day we spent it here in prayers for a plesant tour to ye Painted Rock. Genl McDowell left us this day. He is sick.

27th—A fine pleasant morning set out on the line at 7 o.c. and continued about 1 1/2 miles to the top of a high knob from which the mns appear in every direction high and craggy. The view is wild and romantic, yet the greatest part of the mns through which we passed for some miles back were very rich & covered with rich herbage. The timber generally sugar tree [sugar maple, Acer saccharum] & buckeye…

31st—We had a blustering rainy night; severe lightening & some hard claps of thunder. The company very little the better of their night's rest. Drank a cup of coffee, eat some broiled bacon and Johnny cake, then set out on the line with the prospect of a fine day. Ascended the Stone Mn, continued on the extreme height 6 mi to the Star Gap on ye same where we camped as much fatigued as men could be in going that distance through Lucust thicket, over rocky knobs & narrow ridges almost impassable.

Saturday, June 1. After being much refreshed from our last night's rest we eat a hearty breakfast. Started and continued ye state line along the extreme height of ye Stone Mn in the course of one mile. Seen a very large rattlebug; attempted to kill it, but it was too souple in the heels for us. Continued about 2 m further, took several observations of ye Yellow Mn. Ground very rough. Came to Wattaga River at a very rocky place, crossed on rocks and proceeded near one mile where we encamped on a handsome eminence near a good spring. One of our party turned out and killed a two-year-old she bear. Very poor. Upon which and some bacon stewed together with some good Tea and johnny cake we made a Sabbath breakfast fit for a European Lord…

Thursday, June 6th—A plesant clear morning. Slep sound & comfortable last night. Had no gnats to trouble us. Breakfast on short allowance and set out on the line at 7 o.c. Went about 2 m to the top of the Yellow Mn 1/2 m from ye Yellow spot on a course N.W. by W. at Bright's path, then went to ye Yellow spot in order to take observations, but was disappointed by a hard thunderstorm. The lightning and thunder was so severe that it was truly alarming. The trees at this place is just a-creeping out of there winter's garb…

Saturday, 8th—A pleasant fair morning. We packed up and proceeded on with the line, 4 to 5 m. crossed a high spur of the Roan Mn to a low gap therein where we encamped at a pleasant Beech flat & good spring. Spent the Sabbath day on taking observations from the high spur we crossed, in gathering the fir oil of ye Balsam of Pine [Fraser fir, Abies fraseri] which is found on this mountain, in collecting a root said to be an excellent preventation against the bite of a Rattlesnake, and in viewing the wonderful scenes this conspicuous situation affords. There is no shrubbage grows on the tops of ths Mn for several miles, say 5. The wind has such a power on the top of this mountain that the ground is blowed in deep holes all over the northwest sides. The prospects from the Roan Mn is more conspicuous than from any other part of the Appelatchin Mns…

Wednesday 12th—Spent last night agreeable. Was entertained with some good songs, then slipped ourselves up in our blankets sleep sound till this morning. Arose, eat our breakfast, packed up & started the line. Colo. Vance & Neely went to the Limestone settlement for a Pilot. Returned to us at the line at 2 o.c. with a Mr. Collier Pilot & two gallons whiskey. We stopped, drank our own health & proceeded on the line. Ascended a steep spur of the Unaker Mn. Got into a Laurel thicket, cut our way some distance. Night came on. We turned back and camped at a very bad place, it being a steep Laurelly hollow, but the whiskey had such miraculous powers that it made the place tolerably comfortable…

Friday 21st—Our horses rambled a mile or two from camp, bad range. At length they were collected and at 8 o.c. on the line proceeded on about 3 m to a high Buckeye Ridge to a thick laurelly, narrow rocky ridge, impassable for man or horse. Attempted to go around it, continued 1/2 m through laurel & rocks & encamped at a rocky Br. of Laurel River. No food for our horses; they suffered much for two days past both for water & food…

Thursday 27th—This morning cloudy and hasey. The commissioners being anctous to get on to the Painted Rock started us early. Went on with the line a wrong ridge and fell in another fork of Paint Cr. Returned & encamped on the right ridge where we spent our time uncomfortable this evening.

Friday, 28th—Set out very early and proceeded on the line about 4 m to the painted rock on FB River [French Broad River], about 5 m below the Warm Springs. Measured the height of the rock & found it to be 107 feet 3 inches high from top to the base. It rather projects over the face of the rock; bears but few traces of its having formerly been painted, owing to its having been smoked by pine knots and other wood from a place at its base where travelers have frequently camped. In the year 1790 it was not much smoked; the pictures of some humans, wild beasts, fish & fowls were to be seen plainly made with red paint, some of them 20 & 30 feet from its base.

There is another rock on F.B. River about 7 m higher up on the opposite side or S.W. side in a very obscure place which some gentlemen of Tennessee wish to construe as the painted rock referred to in an act of the Genl. Assembly of No. Carolina entitled an act to cede to the United States certain western lands therein described. But it is to be observed that there is no Rock on French Broad River that ever was known as the painted rock but the one first described, which has ever since the River F. Broad was explored by white men been a place of Publick Notriety.

There may be and I believe there is a rock known by a few Hunters as the paint rock situate about 7 m above the Painted Rock on the S.W. side of French Broad River opposite to an island known by the name of the Mountain Island, but in so obscure a place that but few knows of it & them few only knows it as the paint rock so that it appears to me that the rock first described is unquestionably the rock on F.B. River contemplated by the act of the Genl. Assembly before alluded to. This rock is situated on the N.E. Side of French Broad River just above the mouth of a Cr. Emptying in on ye same side called Paint Creek, from whence the River runs S.W. 10 m then winds to ye N.W. & W 15 M & receives the mouth of Big Pigeon, ect. ect.

We then went up to the Warm Springs where we spent the evening in conviviality and friendship.

Saturday, 29th—The company set out for home to which place I wish them a safe arrival and happy reception. As for myself, I stay at the Springs to get clear of the fatigue of the Tour.

7

JOHN LYON, NURSERYMAN AND PLANT HUNTER, AND HIS JOURNAL, 1799–1814

John Lyon

Following in the footsteps of botanists William Bartram, the father and son team of André and Francois Michaux and John Fraser, and soon to be followed by Thomas Nuttall, Asa Gray and Moses Ashley Curtis, among others, John Lyon (1765–1814) was among the intrepid plant collectors who first penetrated the southern mountains during the late eighteenth and early nineteenth centuries to locate, identify and introduce into cultivation the region's diverse flora. Lyon is among the most neglected botanists of those mentioned. For that reason and because of his close association with the mountains of North Carolina, the biographical note for this selection is lengthier than most others.

Lyon was born in Gillogie in Forfarshire, Scotland. Very little is known about his early life or the events that brought him to the United States. By 1796, he was managing the three-hundred-acre garden of William Hamilton that was located on his Woodlands estate alongside the Schuylkill River just outside Philadelphia. Beginning in 1799, in order to secure additional plants for Woodlands, Lyon was commissioned to make a collecting trip into the Allegheny Mountains of western Pennsylvania. Thereafter, until the year of his death, he made excursions as far west as Nashville and as far south as Florida. Most of his travels, however, were in the southern Appalachians, especially into Western North Carolina, which he visited on seven separate occasions.

The journal Lyon kept is preserved in the American Philosophical Society in Philadelphia. It was edited with extensive notes by Joseph and Nesta Ewan and published in 1963 as "John Lyon, Nurseryman and Plant Hunter, and His Journal, 1799–1814." The journal noted that Lyon collected plants atop several of the region's high peaks, including Roan, Grandfather and Pilot Mountains in North Carolina.

He is credited with introducing more than thirty new plants into cultivation. Among these was fetterbush (*Pieris floribunda*), which he discovered at Pilot Mountain on September 16, 1807. Fetterbush, now planted as far north as Boston because of its hardy nature, is prized for its handsome habit and beautiful early floral displays.

In his informative study *A Reunion of Trees: The Discovery of Exotic Plants and Their Introduction into North American and European Landscapes* (1990), Stephen A. Spongberg

Oil Nut.

recalled that Lyon was the last person to observe and collect the famed Franklin tree (*Franklinia alatamaha*) in the wild. That was on June 1, 1803, when he was exploring the region west of Savannah, Georgia. He recorded in his journal, "It is sufficiently remarkable that this plant has never been found growing naturally in other part of the United States, insofar as I can learn, and here there is not more than 6 or 8 full grown trees of it which do not spread over more than half an acre of ground, the seed has most probably been brought there originally from a great distance by a bird of passage."

Spongberg conjectured, "Demand by nurserymen in England for plants of the Franklin tree may have been largely responsible for its extinction in nature, and Lyon himself may have contributed."

Lyon was unusually successful in transporting living plants to England because he established carefully selected garden sites in the Philadelphia area, where they could be maintained prior to bulk shipment. Although he sometimes, perhaps, had commissions for certain species from wealthy patrons, he primarily sold his stock at auction. Spongberg described a catalogue published by Lyon in 1806 prior to one such auction at Parsons'

Green. It "enumerated 550 lots, and the sale occupied four days. Several of the lots were composed of large quantities of one-year-old seedlings in pots; and ten lots at the end of the sale consisted each of 50 different sorts of seeds."

John Loudon, the Scottish chronicler of arboriculture and agriculture, hailed this shipment in his *Arboretum et Fruticum Brittanicum* (London, 1838) as having been "by far the greatest collection of American trees and shrubs ever brought to England at one time by one individual."

Spongberg, himself a noted collector-naturalist in China and elsewhere, described with sympathy "the risks and privations encountered in the field" by innumerable collectors through the ages. Lyon's situation, in this regard, was extreme:

> *On one foray a mad dog bit the collector on the leg, forcing Lyon to sear the three punctures he sustained with a burning-hot iron and to depend on self-administered folk remedies. When his horse went astray he was sometimes forced to travel on foot, and poor roads and the lack of maps or adequate directions often resulted in lost bearings and restless nights spent without an evening meal and the comfort of a bed. The ultimate disaster that can befall the collector-naturalist in the field is to meet an untimely death, thousands of miles from home, family, and friends. This was the fate of John Lyon.*

His fate was described in a letter written in 1877 by Macon County historian and agriculturist Silas McDowell that was reproduced in F.A. Sondley's *A History of Buncombe County, North Carolina* (1930). McDowell lived as a boy near Asheville from 1912 into 1914. In his letter, McDowell noted that because of a "bilious fever" contracted during his strenuous travels, John Lyon came from Black Mountain in the early autumn of 1814 and took a room in Asheville's Eagle Hotel.

According to McDowell, Lyon and James Johnston—a blacksmith of "almost Herculean" size from Kentucky—had become friends during the botanist's earlier visits to Asheville. When Lyon took to his sickbed, Johnston had another bed placed in the same room for his own use and attended the botanist at night. McDowell had also become attached to Lyon, and on the day of his death went to his room earlier than usual.

Well over half a century later, McDowell recalled,

> *This day had been one of those clear autumnal days when the blue heavens look so transcendently pure! But now the day was drawing fast to a close, the sun was sinking behind the distant blue mountains…The dying man caught a glimpse of the beautiful scene and observed: "Friend Johnston, we are having a beautiful sunset—the last I shall ever behold—will you be so kind as to take me to the window and let me look out?" Johnston carried him to the window took a seat and held the dying man in a position so that his eyes might take in the beautiful scene…After the sun sank out of sight, and the beautiful scene faded out, he exclaimed: "Beautiful world, farewell!"… He fell asleep in a short time and soon all was still. All of John Lyon that was mortal was dead.*

Soon after his death, friends in Edinburgh, Scotland, shipped an engraved tombstone to America that now marks his grave in the Riverside Cemetery in Asheville. There he rests with such luminaries as Thomas Wolfe, William Sydney Porter (O. Henry), Zebulon Baird Vance, Thomas Clingman and George Masa.

From Gillogie in Forfarshire, Scotland, to Asheville in the Carolina mountains—often collecting plants in extreme weather conditions and under dire circumstances—it was for the explorer-nurseryman John Lyon a long, strange journey, one that, for the most part, he apparently reveled in until the very end.

Augt. 16th 1807. Crossed the dividing ridge of mountains between the water and settlements of Keowee [in South Carolina] *and North Carolina and French broad river which is very high being estimated at 6 miles in the ascent from the Eastatowee* [Estatoe] *Settlement to the top, and in many places so steep and rugged that a Horse can hardly clamber up indeed it is in some places very dangerous. Having gained the top of the ridge the path leads along it for several miles comparatively level and in some places no more than 30 or 40 yards wide, while the view on each side to look down is frightful, but the distant view sublime…*

Augt. 27th. Went up with Mr McIntire [who lived twenty-two miles from Asheville] *to the top of the blue ridge near the head spring of the Catawba, on the margin of a remarkable high precepice found the* Rhododendron catawbiense [purple or Catawba rhododendron] *of Mich.* [André Michaux] *as also the* R. punctata [Carolina rhododendron, R. minus]. *Gathered some of the Oil Nuts* [Pyrularia pubera, a small tree or shrub with fruit so oily that it will, according to some sources, "burn like a candle if a wick be drawn through it"] *near the bottom of the ridge…*

Septr. 10th. Remained at Morganton. Packed up seeds of 4 sorts of Magnolias, Oil Nut etc. in a box of moss, and left it in the care of Mr Thos. Walton who promises to send [it] *down to Charleston to be from there sent on the Philadelphia by sea…*

Septr. 15th 1808. Went up Rhoane [Roan] *Mountain with a guide. About 10 oclock began to rain. Lost ourselves for about an hour and a half, owing to the mountains getting covered with mist, in such cases the mountain men frequently get lost, and has no alternative but remain untill* [it] *clears off if they not have a compass with them. With much exersion found our way down a very lucky circumstance as it commenced* [a] *storm which lasted the greater part of three days with torrents of rain, had we not found our way down we probably should have perished before the storm was over with cold and hunger which probably would been the fate of our horses also as we left them penned up at the bottom of the mountain so that they could not have shifted for themselves. Got back to the settlements which is 9 miles from the bottom of the mountain at dusk extremely fatigued & wet. The mountain is generally a fine rich soil with large growing trees of various sorts of Oaks, Walnuts, etc. which constitutes to a certain elevation or distance up the mountain when the same species suddenly assumes a more dwarf stunted appearance, and gradually diminishes in height as we ascend untill they become stunted dwarfs so that we can scarce get under their branches, a little higher they mix more with shrubs of a humble growth making a sort of ring of thicket difficult to get through when they altogether terminate. Then commences what the mountain people call the bald grounds* [grassy balds], *these are the highest summits of the highest mountains and are in many instances comparatively level grounds of very considerable extent, soil deep and rich producing fine grass and herbage more like that of natural meadows than mountains, with a few clumps of Vacciniums* [blueberry and related plants] *and other shrubs but of very humble growth interspersed. Probably the reason that nothing of the tree kind grows on these bold grounds is cold, or the action of the wind, or perhaps both these causes combined owing to their great elevation or height. It is sufficiently remarkable that this highest mountains are alwise the richest soil. They will probably one day become some of the finest sheep pastures in the world…*

Octr. 23rd. Remained at Asheville. Clear and plesent. Having been unable to travel for nearly three weeks on account of an inflamation in my left leg which seems now so far subsided as to admit of going on I have for the last two or three days been preparing for a Journey through the Pigeon Settlements, and the Cherokee Mountains…

Octr. 28th. Commensed our Journey through the Cherokee mountains…Crossed the Tucasigee [Tuckasegee River] *a consider*[able] *stream the north branch of the* [Little] *Tennessee and several smaller streams branches of the same river passed by Kuloage/Sugar Town/*[situated on the Cullasaja River in present Macon County] *which is now nearly deserted, and a few other settlements of the Indians. The path this days Journey has been through a rough mountainous tract of country…*

Octr. 29th. Got on to Alexr. Carls a white man married to a half breed. Distance about 25 miles. A considerable part of this days Journey has been along the main branch of the [Little] *Tennessee a considerable and beautifull stream on each side of the river is fine level natural meadows of considerable width with very* [few] *trees or shrub producing fine natural grass, and a great variety of herbaceous plants, and would if cultivated be very productive. Passed through several settlements of the Indians. Gathered seed etc.*

8

DIARY OF A GEOLOGICAL TOUR
BY DR. ELISHA MITCHELL
IN 1827 AND 1828

Elisha Mitchell

Geologist, teacher, minister and explorer, Elisha Mitchell (1793–1857) was a native of Washington, Connecticut. Several years after graduating from Yale University in 1813, he received an appointment as a professor at the University of North Carolina, where he served in various capacities for the rest of his life.

"His great self-reliance caused his death," noted Dr. Kemp P. Battle in the biographical note written for the seventy-three-page pamphlet from which this selection is excerpted.

> *He claimed to have visited the highest peak of the Black Mountains. General Thomas L. Clingman contended that he himself was the first discoverer and endeavored to have it called Mount Clingman. After a long controversy in the newspapers, Dr. Mitchell determined to ascertain the height by the spirit level, as he had formerly done by the barometer. On the 27th of June, 1857…he endeavored to ascend the mountain alone and go down on the Yancey [County] side, in order to visit one or more of his former guides. Being detained by a thunderstorm it was late in the afternoon when he began to descend a fork of Caney river. By the side of a forty-foot precipice he slipped and fell into a deep pool below. His body was not found until the eighth of July. He was buried in Asheville, but the next year his family allowed his body to be buried on [the* peak eventually recognized as] *Mount Mitchell.*

In 1881 and 1882, the U.S. Geological Survey confirmed Mitchell's measurement, which, at 6,684 feet, is the highest peak east of the Rockies. It was officially named in his honor. Thomas Clingman's compensation was already in place—in 1860, Clingmans Dome in the Great Smokies, at 6,642 feet the second highest peak in the East, had been named for him.

In the late 1820s, Mitchell was continuing the geological survey of North Carolina initiated in 1824. Intrigued by John Calhoun's assertion that the southern Appalachians contained peaks higher than any others east of the Mississippi River, he focused his attention for the first time on the western portion of the state.

Fraser Fir.

Diary of a Geological Tour by Dr. Elisha Mitchell in 1827 and 1828 was published by the University of North Carolina as a "James Sprunt Historical Monograph" in 1905. The so-called "diary" actually consists of letters written by Mitchell to his wife, Maria. It was compiled and edited by Dr. Kemp P. Battle, also of the University of North Carolina, who received the materials from Mitchell's granddaughter, Margaret Mitchell, in 1903. The first letter was dated December 28, 1827—the last August 3, 1828.

> *Sales', 15 miles east of Wilkesboro, Thursday evening* [July 1828].
> *…The country traversed today is fertile but much less beautiful than that through which I passed yesterday. Something raw and countrified about it. Still I am coming in among the mountains, and the Blue Ridge is in full view from this place—a part of Ashe* [County]…

> *Foot of the Blue Ridge at Mrs. Colberts, Friday Evening.*
> *…I crossed the Yadkin by fording, traveled over mica slate chiefly, crossed some impure plumbago* [graphite] *at six miles, at nine miles descended into the valley of Reddie's river* [Reddy Branch], *and traveled by the side of it until quite near this. These four miles were very pleasant—the steep mountains were on either hand—the river clear as crystal tumbled over its rocky bed, and there were fine fields of corn upon its banks. The farms are small and here, according to some men calling themselves philosophers, in retirement shut out from intercourse with the world by the sides of these streams*

Diary of a Geological Tour by Dr. Elisha Mitchell in 1827 and 1828

and hemmed in by these mountains—man may, if he will, be happy. But they are less happy than we…

Jefferson, Saturday Evening.
Arrived at this place about noon in safety. Fox has not yet run away with me. Indeed, there seems more danger that the crows will run away with him. The poor old fellow is badly worsted. His back is very sore, and I shall leave him here on Monday and hire a horse to ride about the country with…Seven miles from the top of the ridge after a moderate descent—the path apparently over mica slate almost exclusively—only two or three houses; I came to New River. It is a beautiful stream, broad but not deep, clear and running its course among the mountains, which often over hang its banks and overshadow its waters…I ascended the highest of the mountains in the neighborhood along with Mr. Faw, and a rugged ascent it was. Saw a good many plants that were new to me, dug a root of ginseng for you, a small one with my own hands. The air being clear, the prospect delightful. The Pilot [Mountain] could be distinguished clearly, probably at the distance of near a hundred miles. It appeared to be almost exactly east. The Grandfather, or the mountain which we supposed to be the one bearing that name, bore S. 40 west. We had a clear view of the country lying down the New River in Virginia, and also of the part of Surry, Wilkes, etc., lying near the Blue Ridge, for the point on which we were standing was high enough to overlook the Blue Ridge. Nearly the whole county of Ashe lay at our feet, the Merry-anders [annotated by Battle as "a jocular way of writing meanders"] of the river could be traced as on a map. Some of the plantation in view also presented a noble appearance, but oh, what an ocean of mountains…

Thursday morning.
John Weaver came in before I was up to have me determine some ore for him, and agreed to go with me to the Whitetop, an exceedingly high mountain, 3 miles north of the, say Northwestern most corner of N.Ca. of course in Virginia. Went out to see Perkins' ore bank which is extensive and then while breakfast was getting ready heard an amusing account of an old man who determined the locality of ores by the mineral rod, and by his own account is very busy in digging for gold and silver taken from the White by the Indians, and laid up in "subteranium chambers." Said he greased his boots with dead men's tallow, and is prevented from getting the treasure out not by the little spirit with head not bigger than his two thumbs who come to blow the candle out, but by the great old two horned devil himself. After breakfast wound over the hills to William Perkins, then up Helton 2 miles along a new horse path and by an old plantation to John Weavers. He has a wonderfully romantic place by the side of the creek under the over-hanging rocks. He is a bachelor of 27. His sister keeps house for him. Another house appeared at the distance of two miles up the creek, and we were apprised of our approach by the rolling of drums which the boys kept to frighten away the cattle that are driven in here in great numbers from Washington county, and eat up the range. Being very wild the drum scares them so that they go heels over head down

the sides of the mountain; and a 4 year old ox will clear a 2 year old ox at a single bound…

Sunday Morning.
…Preached at 12 to a considerably attentive congregation. After dinner rode down 10 miles to Watauga. Smith purchased a bottle of brandy and put it in my saddlebags. The prospect in some places where the chestnuts now in bloom grow upon rich grounds on the declivities of the mountains, and are covered with a most luxuriant foliage, is enchanting…

Monday Morning.
…We had still 8 or 9 miles to go to the top of Grandfather. We passed on over one ridge after another winding through the woods over logs and rocks, and through laurels, walking when we could not ride, passing some mountains and knobs with very indecent names, seeing only one small deer which we did not kill, crossing the head of Linville river, which flows into the Catawba, and arrived at the foot of Grandfather, where we were obliged to leave our horses about one o'clock. The Linville and Watauga head up under the mountain, and from the place, where we took our dinner we could get water from either, within two or three hundred yards. Of course we were on the summit of the Blue Ridge. The ascent of the mountain is rough, thickety and disagreeable. Steep, perpendicular cliffs in places but in general not very difficult. About half way up we met with a Fir-Balsam tree [Fraser fir, *Abies fraseri*]. *It is sometimes a foot and a half in thickness and pretty tall. The balsam resides in small blisters or cavities in the substance of the bark which are cut out as the precious fluid passed into a vial.* [This fluid is an oleoresin, a mixture of an essential oil and a resin.] *They say that the exudation obtained in the same way as common turpentine has not the same properties—but I have my doubts. It is the panacea or universal remedy of the mountains—cures wounds, rheumatism, flux, et cetera. It grows quite to the top but it is stunted and smaller there, and along with one other tree* [red spruce, *Picea rubens*] *occupies exclusively the highest points.* [Another description of the Fraser fir appears in the selection by Henry E. Colton.] *The summit of the mountain is moist and wet, producing carexes* [sedges] *which I wished to but could not study. Holtsclaw had been often upon it but only in search of bears of which it is the favorite winter retreat. They retire to dens in the cliffs in December and come out in February, passing the time in sleep. This is time for the hunters to find their retreats and take them out. They lose nothing of their fatness, and their flesh is thought to acquire additional delicacy; they have nothing in their bowels during their sleep—I write this at Jefferson, July 11, Friday. I leave today for the lower end of the county where I hope to go out to the Elkspur Gap on Saturday into Wilkes…*

Elkspur Gap, Wilkes Co., July 20th. 1828.
My Dear and Good Wife:
Amongst the unpleasant circumstances with which my present occupation is attended is the inability under which I am laid of spending the Sabbath in a manner which my

*conscience approves. As I am laid up here for a day with no good books at hand and as
your situation is desolate—and lonely (but still how different from that of a widowed
mother), I believe I may regard it as a duty as well as feel it a pleasure to resume my
narrative at the point where it was broken off upon the summit of the Grandfather and
fill a sheet and a half (you cannot in conscience complain as I have nearly exhausted
all the paper which you gave me) with ulterior particulars. It is one of the pleasures of
the relation in which we stand to each other that those trifles which to a third person
would be intolerably wearisome have with us a deep as well as unfailing interest. You
must excuse repetition if I should happen to fall into any.*

*The vegetation of the summit of the Grandfather is peculiar. Carexes (inhabitants
of a moist soil) constitute the principal grasses, the trees are the Balsam Fir—and
one or two others which I did not know. Does not Michaux assign to this mountain a
peculiar species of Pine* [table mountain pine, *Pinus pungens*] *not found elsewhere
upon the Mountain? I could see nothing of any such and Henry Holtsclaw denied
that there was any. Saw a new (to me) species of sambucus* [red-berried elder,
Sambucus pubens, which is toxic] *with red berries which were already ripe and at the
point where we enjoyed the first prospect a small shrub grew and interwove its branches
so thick that we reposed upon the summit of its limbs as upon a carpet. The climate
of the summit must be considerably colder than that of Chapel Hill as the Blackberry,
which I found fully ripe in many places as I came along before I reached the foot of the
Mountain and were decaying through excessive ripeness, was still green throughout Ashe
at this time and near the summit of the Grandfather was either flowering or passing
into the state of berry. Capt. Smith, who had worn his thin coat up, complained bitterly
of the coldness of the wind and I felt it myself though less than he did. To enjoy
the prospect in all its glory we climbed each a several Balsam tree and the tree being
stunted in its growth had a large trunk (comparatively) thickly beset with limbs so that
we could easily place our heads higher than its top. The prospect was all but infinite.
The day was fine—a few flying clouds and a thin haze or smoke only. The Pilot
and several towns were distinctly visible, also endless ridges of Tennessee, the Black
Mountain of Buncombe, the Yellow and Roan Mountains. The Table rock which
appeared as a considerable eminence at Morganton was dwindled down to a Mole Hill.
It was a question with us whether the Black and Roan Mountains were not higher than
the Grandfather and we were all inclined to give them the palm and I very well recollect
that when I was in Morganton last year a mountain lying towards the westward
appeared higher than it and the same impression was made by the Yellow and Roan
mountains when I was upon the White Top. There can be no doubt that the country
around the base of the Grandfather is higher than any other tract along these elevations
but I suspect the Black and Roan to be higher peaks. The Grandfather appears to
me to be Grau Wacke* [greywacke, a conglomerate or grit rock, consisting
of rounded pebbles and sand firmly united together] *and to belong to the
transition of Tennessee. Along the creek by which we ascended I found clay slate which
appeared to be in transition—also about the very head springs of Linnville and along
the flank of the Grandfather. If I am correct I suspect that instead of there being a*

small strip of transition along the base of the Blue Ridge as represented by Maclure [Scottish geologist William Maclure] that formation here occupies the whole breadth of the Mountains. If I were to spend another summer in these parts I would locate myself on the Old Fields of Toe River and investigate the district lying between and around these high mountains. When we had finished our examination we began to descend in a great hurry it being the object of the hunters to reach the cabin of Mr. Leatherstocking Aldridge and feast upon Venison, Bear Meat and Honey. In the attempt to do this we failed and camped on the top of Haw Ridge three miles from Barnhills. A shelving rock projected over our heads and kept off the dew; my blanket, after it had served as a manger for my horse to eat his provender from, constituted a bed for Henry Holtsclaw and Robert Barnhill. My Buffalo skin served Capt. John Smith whilst my bearskin served Mr. Noah Mast and myself. Thus furnished I lying in the middle and with a blazing fire at our feet we passed a pleasanter night than I had expected. I looked at my watch a good many times to see if it was not nearly morning.

9

LETTERS FROM THE
ALLEGHANY MOUNTAINS (1849)

Charles Lanman

Writer, librarian, artist and explorer Charles Lanman (1819–1895) was born in Monroe, Michigan. He was the grandson of Senator James Lanman of Connecticut. His father, James Lanman, moved west to the Territory of Michigan from New England to practice law. In 1829, Charles was sent back east to his grandfather to be educated. Lanman's long and varied professional career included stints at a mercantile house in New York City, as the editor of several newspapers, as an associate of the National Academy of Design (he specialized in oil paintings from nature), as the private secretary of Daniel Webster, as a librarian (at the War Department, Interior Department, House of Representatives and Washington City Library) and as American secretary of the Japanese legation for ten years.

Lanman published thirty-two books during his lifetime, including *The Private Life of Daniel Webster* (1952), *Personal Memoirs of Daniel Webster* (1953) and *Dictionary of the United States Congress* (1859). He also edited and contributed to *The Japanese in America* (1872).

According to the *Dictionary of American Biography*, it was in the mid-1830s that Lanman began "exploring places in the eastern part of the United States, then more difficult of access, which have since become well-known vacation resorts. He was one of the first to use the canoe as a pleasure craft." By the 1840s, "his fishing trips and explorations on foot, on horseback, and in canoes carried him through the Mississippi Valley, the region of the Great Lakes and the St. Lawrence, and over the whole of the Appalachian system from the Bay of Fundy to the Gulf States."

Lanman submitted articles describing these trips and exploits to various magazines. He then revised and gathered the articles to compile books such as *A Summer in the Wilderness* (1847), *Adventures of an Angler in Canada, Nova Scotia and the United States* (1848), *A Tour to the River Saguenay* (1849), *Letters from the Alleghany Mountains* (1849) and *Haw-ho-noo, or Records of a Tourist* (1850). These were so popular that a collected edition was initially published in London under the title *Adventures in the Wilds of North America* (1854) and then, with additions, in Philadelphia (two volumes) as *Adventures in the Wilds of the United States and British American Provinces* (1856).

Panther.

In this selection from *Letters from the Alleghany Mountains*, Lanman traveled east from Murphy through the large alluvial bottomlands along the Valley River where Andrews is situated. (The mountains of Western North Carolina and adjacent regions were often referred to as the "Allegheny Mountains" during the nineteenth century. Lanman used the variant spelling "Alleghany.") He then crossed over the upper Nantahala River (where there is a small gorge system with vertical cliffs) and the Nantahala Mountains to reach Franklin. He apparently did not penetrate the Nantahala Gorge proper (now famous for whitewater rafting and related activities) in the lower reaches of the river.

It is now generally agreed that the Cherokee word "Nantahala" or "Nan-ti-ha-la"—which Lanman suggests can be translated as "woman's bosom"—actually means something closer to "Land-of-the-Noonday-Sun," in reference to the fact that the lower gorge is so deep sunlight only penetrates it for a few hours each day, especially in winter.

In this selection, Lanman recorded several panther stories related to him by residents of the area. Even though panthers (also called cougars or mountain lions) were supposedly extirpated from Western North Carolina and the Great Smokies by 1920, they would have been fairly common in the remote Nantahala Mountains in the late 1840s.

The distance from Murphy to Franklin village is reported to be fifty miles. For twenty miles the road runs in full view of Valley river, which is worthy in every particular of the stream into which it empties, the Owassa [the Hiwassee River]. *It is a remarkably cold and translucent stream, and looks as if it ought to contain trout…*

After leaving the above valley, my course lay over two distinct spurs of the Alleghanies, which are divided by the river Nan-ti-ha-lah, and consequently called the Nan-ti-ha-lah Mountains. In ascending the western ridge, I noticed that at the foot and midway up the pass the trees were all arrayed in their summer verdure, and among the forest trees were many chestnut and poplar specimens, which were at least seven or eight feet in diameter; while the more elevated portions of the ridge were covered with scrub and white oak, which were entirely destitute of foliage and not even in the budding condition. No regular cliffs frowned upon me as I passed along, but the mountains on either side were almost perpendicular, and in one or two places were at least twenty-five hundred feet high. In the side of the highest of these mountains, I was informed, is a deep fissure or cave, which extends to the summit of the hill, where the outlet is quite small. When the wind is blowing from the northwest it passes entirely through this long and mysterious cavern, and when issuing from the top comes with such force as to throw out all the smaller stones which one may happen to drop therein. In descending this spur, the road passes directly along the margin of the most gloomy thicket imaginable. It is about a mile wide and somewhat over three miles in length. It is rank with vegetation, and the principal trees are laurel, pine, and cedar [eastern hemlock?]. *Even at noonday it is impossible to look into it more than half a dozen yards, and then you but peer into the opening of leafy caves and grottos which are perpetually cool and very desolate. It is said to abound in the more ferocious of wild animals, and no white man is yet known to have mustered courage enough to explore the jungle. During the existence of the Cherokee difficulties* [the Cherokee removal era culminated in 1838 with the deportation of sixteen thousand tribal members to Oklahoma], *the Indians were in the habit of encamping on many places on its margin for the purpose of easily eluding their pursuers; and it is reported of one Indian hunter, who once entered the thicket, that he never returned, having, as is supposed, been overpowered by some wild beast. It was upon the margin of this horrible place, too, that the following incident occurred: An Indian woman once happened to be travelling down the mountain, unaccompanied by her husband, but with three young children, two little girls and a papoose. In an unexpected moment an enraged panther crossed their trail,* and while it fell upon and destroyed the mother and one child, the elder girl ran for her life, carrying the infant on her back. The little heroine had not gone over a half a mile with her burden before the panther caught up with her, and dragged the infant from her grasp; and while the savage creature was destroying this third victim, the little girl made her escape to a neighboring encampment.

The river Nan-ti-ha-lah, or the Woman's Bosom, was so named on account of its undulating and narrow valley, and its own intrinsic purity and loveliness. Upon this river is situated a rude but comfortable cabin, which is the only one the traveller meets with in going a distance of twenty miles. On first approaching this cabin, I noticed a couple of sweet little girls playing on the greensward before the door with a beautiful fawn, which was as tame as a lamb. This group, taken in connection with the wildness of the surrounding scene, gave me a most delightful feeling, the contrast was so strange and unexpected. The proprietor of the cabin owns about five thousand acres of land in this wilderness region, and is by profession a grazing farmer. He raises a goodly number of cattle as well as horses and mules, and his principal markets for them are Charleston and Savannah, to which cities he performs a pilgrimage in the autumn of every year. He is one of the "oldest inhabitants" of the region, and as I spent one night under his roof, I took occasion to draw from him a few anecdotes connected with his own experience. On questioning him with regard to the true character of the panther, he replied as follows: "I don't know much about this animal, but I have had one chance to study their nature, which I can't forget. It was a very dark night, and I was belated on the western ridge, near the Big Laurel ravine. I was jogging along at a slow rate, when my horse made a terrible leap aside, and I saw directly in front of me one of the biggest of panthers. It soon uttered a shriek or scream (which sounded like a woman in distress) and got out of the way, so that I could pass along. Every bone in my horse's body trembled with fear, and I can tell you that my own feelings were pretty squally. On my way was I still jogging, when the panther again made his appearance, just as he had before, and gave another of his infernal yells. I had no weapon with me, and I now thought I was a gone case. Again did the animal disappear, and again did I continue on my journey. I had not gone more than a hundred yards before I saw, on the upper side of the road, what looked like a couple of balls of fire, and just as I endeavored to urge my horse a little faster, another dreadful scream rang far down the valley. But, to make a long story short, this animal followed me until I got within a half a mile of my house, and, though he ran around me at least a dozen times, and uttered more than a dozen screams, he never touched me, and I got safely home. If you can gather any information from this adventure you are welcome to it; but all I know about the animal is this, that I hate him as I do the devil."

10

MOUNTAIN SCENERY (1859)

Henry E. Colton

Naturalist, geologist and author Henry E. Colton (1836–1892) was born in Fayetteville, North Carolina. He was the son of the Reverend Simeon Colton, a native of Somers, Connecticut, who moved to Fayetteville in 1833 to act as headmaster of Donaldson Academy. Colton's career can be summarized as follows: work in a printing office, possibly in Wilmington or in Asheville; editor of the weekly *Asheville Spectator* during the late 1850s; publication in 1859 of *Mountain Scenery* and, in 1860, of the sixteen-page *Guide Book to the Scenery of Western North Carolina*; private in the Thirty-sixth Regiment of North Carolina Troops and later the Thirteenth Battalion of North Carolina Light Artillery during the Civil War; editorial staff of the *New York Tribune* while Horace Greeley was editor; mining engineer (apparently in Tennessee); and state geologist of Tennessee. Identifying himself as "Henry E. Colton, Geologist and Inspector of Mines," he also published several books on coal mining and steel ore. He was buried in Knoxville, Tennessee, where he is believed to have been in residence for a number of years.

Colton contributed numerous articles to various Southern newspapers as well as to well-known magazines of the period such as the *Southern Literary Messenger* and the *Southern Quarterly Review*. Five lengthy articles on the French Broad River were contributed to *Appletons' Journal* between November 1870 and May 1871 as part of that publication's "Picturesque America" series are of special interest.

His most significant literary accomplishment—published when he was but twenty-one years old—was *Mountain Scenery*. Often categorized as "the first tourist guidebook to Western North Carolina," it was the first book containing significant amounts of nature and descriptive writing that was devoted almost entirely to the mountainous districts of North Carolina. Colton no doubt added "Northwestern South Carolina" to the title to sell additional copies, but very little of the text is descriptive of that state. Unfortunately, the book is now quite rare and inordinately expensive when advertised for sale. However, a handsome online edition—one that reproduces all of the illustrations and the full text—is available in the University of North Carolina at Chapel Hill's "Documenting the American South" collection of electronic editions (see the Colton bibliographic entry).

Linville Falls.

The illustrations in *Mountain Scenery* were lithographs executed by Herline & Hensel Lithographers, the prestigious nineteenth-century Philadelphia firm operated by Edward Herline and Daniel Hensel. Their lithographs were rendered on stone treated so that non-image areas would not retain ink. The final result was an evocative, almost painterly, illustration. It is not known who prepared the sketches or paintings that the lithographs were based upon. The illustration's titles are indicative of their subject matter: "View of Asheville NC and the Mountains from the Beaux Catcher Knob"; "Hickory Nut Falls: Height of

Uninterrupted Fall 350 Feet, Height of Precipice 900 Ft, This Stream in the Foreground is Broad River"; "Mitchell's Falls"; and "View of the Pilot Mountain from Mr. Gillam's."

Colton's book consisted of fifteen chapters and an appendix. Chapter XV described "Productions of the West, Agricultural and Mineral—Wild Flowers—Tree Growth—Wild Animals and Reptiles." The remaining fourteen chapters and the appendix described routes travelers could follow to access and explore particular localities in Western North Carolina, from east of Asheville to Murphy in the southwestern corner of the state. For example, chapters are headed in this manner: "The Hickory Nut Gap Route"; "The Vicinity of Asheville—The White Sulphur Springs—The Million Springs—Pleasant Drives"; "The Roan Mountain—The Great Bald Mountain"; "The French Broad River and the Warm Springs"; and so on. This selection is from a chapter in which Colton viewed Linville Falls and then described his exploration of "a cave"— that is, Linville Caverns.

There here are numbers of natural curiosities throughout the South which are never seen or heard of except by some adventurous traveller, and known intimately only by the intrepid mountain hunter. Thus, these curiosities remain unnoted, while yearly thousands of our citizens go northwards in search of pleasure. Among such may be classed the Falls of the Linville River, in Burke County. We doubt not but numbers of persons in Burke County never heard of them. They are to be found in the northwest corner of that county, near to that famous tree upon which the four counties of Burke, Watauga, Yancey, and McDowell corner, and about nine miles from the Piedmont Springs. The facilities for getting to them are as yet about no facilities at all; an idea may be formed from our experience...

Following our guide, we seated ourself on the top of a rock, around the base of which the river rushes in its wild career. About forty feet below us, on one side, dashed the troubled waters of the Linville; on the other, these same waters having forced themselves through a passage not more than ten feet here, made their descent over the last and highest fall...Our position was a commanding one, but not such as a person with weak nerves should seek. As we gazed far down the course of the river, we could see the stream again assume its comparatively placid appearance; but now, instead of banks almost even with its bed, it was locked in by an impenetrable mass of chimney rocks, which continue for miles down its course, rising in the most majestic grandeur to a height of one, two, and three hundred feet, and in some places near to a thousand. At one point we are informed the rocks close over the river, and it is easy for a person to jump from one bank to the other.

The grand sublimity of the scenery which is hereabouts presented to the eye, cannot be surpassed by any in the world. Language fails to describe it, and the pencil of the artist can give but a faint conception of its beauty and magnificent grandeur. Here it is that man feels his insignificance and trembling kneels with awe and fear. We have seen Niagara in all its artistic splendor, and we have seen what was called grand scenery, but never, never, have we seen anything to equal the scenery of Linville Falls, nor do we ever expect to see the like again until we revisit them.

On Tuesday morning, I left the house to explore a cave in the limestone formation, which was the chief object of my visit there. Having procured a guide, a little after 9 o'clock we entered the cave, and after proceeding about a quarter of a mile, came to water. Previous to this, nothing of a very remarkable nature had met with, but now began the wondrous splendors of that hidden world. Stooping through a low passage, in which the coldest of water ran rippling and singing a merry song, which echoed back a thousand times from the dark dismal arched roof of the unmeasured space which stretched itself before, behind, and above us, we emerged into an immense passage, whose roof was far beyond the reach of the glare of our torches, except where the fantastic festoons of stalactites hang down within our touch. It looked like the arch of some grand old cathedral, yet it was too sublime, too perfect in all its beautiful proportions, to be anything of human, but a model which man might attempt to imitate. Passing along we would come to a huge figure, so horridly like the petrified skeleton of a human being, that as the fitful glimmering light cast a shade upon it, one would start back in horror. But a steadier shade exhibits it truly to our sight—nought but the working of nature, yet so perfect in its lineaments that it would take no great stretch of the imagination to think it a petrified remnant of the body of one of that departed race of giants, which fables tell us once strode over the land. Revelling in these horrid phantasies of the imagination, I touched it. How cold—icy cold! My hand was numbed by the contact. But I missed my guide, and turning, I noticed him far above me, ascending a kind of natural stairs. I soon followed, and through a hole, hardly large enough for my body, entered a chamber, which, in the gorgeous splendor of its transparent drapery, the beauty and delicate look of its carpeting, surpassed any natural scene I ever witnessed. I thought to myself that could one but hear the strains of delicious music, he might well conclude that the land of the fairies was reached at last. It was not a large, gross cavern, with dark, gloomy stalactites, but these pendants were of a delicate lightness, and a most beautifully transparent yellowish hue, while the floor was covered with a formation which more resembled white moss petrified than anything else I can compare it to. My guide was pushing himself about into the various passages far from me, and not a sound reached me but the sweet murmur of the rippling water, which, as it came echoing along through the thousand harp-strings which hang from the roofing, answered my imagination amply for the music of the fairy elfs, while my torch giving but light enough to illumine the little room in which I sat, allowed my mind's eye to see hundreds of shapes dancing merrily in the thick darkness below. Had I but a picture of that scene, it should be an heirloom which I would pride in transmitting to an after generation, for I am convinced that never man stood on that spot before. Far beyond, half hanging on a ledge of rock, was my guide, looking more like a goblin from another world than a mortal creature of this, his face blackened with lightwood smoke, and his clothes covered with mud, his light held high above him, and his head stretched out in a searching glance into the pitchy darkness of a cavern which lay before him. Soon satisfied that he could see about as far as the end of his nose, he seized a rock and struck a huge stalactite near him, bringing forth a deafening, crashing sound, which, echoing through a hundred passages, rang like a chime of bells, and thus dispelled a fancy of mine whereby I was endeavoring to make him out a giant spirit of the goblin world. Soon with a bound or two he reached me, and announced the not very astounding fact that it was farther than he had ever been before, and that no one had ever been farther than he. His next was, "Shall we go on?" To which I replied, "To the end." And on we went, sometimes in water up to our knees, then beside the stream as it rippled on, now stooping or crawling through a narrow passage, again standing erect in a vast arched chamber, hung with the grandest of nature's stony tapestry. Every little while we would turn aside and examine some finely adorned chamber, whose splendid carvings would so dazzle the eye that the last seemed always the most beautiful. At length my guide cried, "Look out for your light!" and well I heard it, for just then my foot slipped, and I was in a pool of water about four feet deep, and about as near ice as I ever wish to see that element. As I was in, I kept on, holding a ledge of rock so as not to go any deeper, and soon the narrow passage opened into a good-sized chamber, and the cave proper was at an end. There were several passages branching out, but all very small and difficult of access.

Then I sat down on a sort of artificial seat which extended round the pool, which seemed to constitute the head of the stream of water we had been tracing, and thought for the first time of the peril I was in. But yet it did not seem to me as if there was anything to fear. There we were, under the centre of the Humpback Peak of the Blue Ridge, with at least 2500 feet of rock and earth above us, in a place where the foot of man had never before trod, with nothing but our own intelligence to tell us the road back, and how much that may have been bewildered, we know not. At length we turned our steps backward, and, after travelling rapidly for some time, reached the mouth of the cave. I suppose the length we went to could not have been less than a mile. The water has a slight taste of lime, and runs with great rapidity, occasionally standing in pools of some depth. About three or four hundred yards from the mouth of the cave it turns directly south, and sinks into the rock after a short distance. I found, far in the cave, a perfect grasshopper, petrified and covered with a crust of lime. We found bats, and traces of mice. So great was the change in the atmosphere, from the cave to open air, that all my clothing dried without the aid of fire…

This work of nature can, probably, be visited with less expense than any other noted spot in the West. It is impossible exactly to estimate the cost, as all depends on the number of the party, and the time spent there. The general charges are, however, about fifty cents for a man and horse one night.

11

A WEEK IN THE GREAT SMOKY MOUNTAINS (1860)

R., of Tennessee

A Week in the Great Smoky Mountains" was published in 1860 in the *Southern Literary Messenger*, which during an impressive thirty-year run (1834–64) was the South's most important literary periodical. Published in Richmond, Virginia, the monthly magazine was edited in its early years by Edgar Allan Poe. In addition to serving as a literary proving ground for Poe, it is also remembered for publishing poems, fiction and essays by some of the nation's leading authors—both male and female, Northern and Southern—including William Gilmore Simms, Paul Hamilton Hayne, Joseph G. Baldwin, John Pendleton Kennedy, Mary E. Lee and Caroline Lee Hentz.

The identity of "R., of Tennessee" is unknown, but his motivation for making this excursion into the Great Smoky Mountains seventy-four years before the area became a national park is clear enough. Because of a condition R. described as "hemmorage of the lungs," his physician recommended "vigorous out-door exercise in a cold, bracing climate" like that in Minnesota. Not wanting to travel so far, R. chose instead to sojourn in the nearby Smokies. Praising the physician for being one of the few men "in the healing profession who believes in God and nature," R. at first "tried in vain to get anyone to accompany me to the mountains." Unable to locate a companion, the writer determined to go alone.

> *Upon Thursday, 3rd of November, 1859, I left Knoxville, the capital of East Tennessee, upon horse-back, taking with me two blankets, an over-coat, in one pocket of which there was a pint flask of the best brandy, a pair of saddlebags, in one side of which I had stuffed two or three pairs of socks and as many shirts, and a copy of Dr. Draper's Physiology, and in the other side, to make the balance even, a quart bottle of the same article with which the pint flask was filled. Of course I did not mean to use the quart of brandy, for then the saddlebags would have lost their balance and fallen off.*

R. journeyed from Knoxville to Sevierville and then up the Little Pigeon River on the Tennessee side of what is now the Great Smoky Mountains National Park, seeking

Peregrine Falcon.

a high mountain peak he called "Quonacatoosa." This was Clingmans Dome, which he wrongly supposed to be "by far the loftiest elevation east of the Rocky Mountains." We join him deep in the mountains as he is making his way on foot to the Alum Cave, a dramatic overhang that is to this day the destination (or way station along the trail to Mount Le Conte) of thousands of visitors to the national park each year. It is named for the presence of minerals once referred to as alums (really pseudo-alums) that—along with Epsom salts, saltpeter and other materials—were mined there during the nineteenth century. We leave him just above Alum Cave at a forlorn site situated not very far below "the crest of the mountains on the dividing line between Tennessee and North Carolina."

Sunday, 6ᵗʰ Nov—Jack Bradley [R.'s locally-hired guide] *made his appearance this morning before breakfast, and of course before sunrise, ready to start to Alum Cave with me. Jack carried his gun and a blanket, a hand axe and a sack filled with provisions—for you see we intended to stay all night and next day in the mountains…It is useless to attempt to describe the wild and romantic scenery through which we passed. We spent the whole day through laurel thickets, with no path to guide us, passed over rapid mountain torrents by springing from rock to rock, many times at places where I should have never thought of attempting, had not Jack gone before, and at about two o'clock arrived at Alum Cave, thoroughly and utterly exhausted by our toilsome climbing and walk of seven miles. The last half mile was nearly perpendicular. I do not believe I could possibly have held out to climb one hundred yards more. I threw myself on the ground in the entrance of Alum Cave. As I lay there panting, Jack took one of the blankets and threw it over me, reminding me that it was very cold up there, and that I would certainly make myself sick if I cooled off too rapidly…*

Well here we are at Alum Cave! Some five or six thousand feet up in the air. A wilder, grander spot I never saw before. It is not strictly a cave, it is what is called in the mountains "a rock-house,"—that is, a precipice so far projecting over its base, as to shelter the space beneath from rain and snow. At Alum Cave the projection is so great that it may well be called a cave. On the brow of the overhanging cliff above there are quite a number of eagle's nests. They live there all the time, Jack told me. I saw several careering about, and heard others screaming among the rocks above. I was reminded of Mccaulay's lines in Horatius: "Like an eagle's nest hangs on the crest/Of purple Appenine!" I hope they may never be disturbed or driven away—'twould almost be treason to our flag to do so. [R.'s "eagles" were undoubtedly peregrine falcons, which nested at Duckhawk Ridge in the vicinity of the Alum Cave until the early 1940s. They did not return to breed there again until the spring of 1997.]

At the lower edge or end of the cave is what is called "Devil's Leap." This is a cliff which, though not quite perpendicular, must be one thousand feet to the bottom. The very thought of taking such a leap almost makes one's hair stand on end. At the upper edge of the cave, the precipice closes quite down to the side of mountain below, so that progress in that direction is impossible. Just to the west of the cave arises another rugged mountain peak, whose sides are so steep no one has yet been able to climb to the top of it…Through the sides of this beetling cliff are great holes, and give the cliff a very peculiar and grand appearance…

Having wandered about for an hour or two in the cave, I left, with regret, just before sun-down, to find some water at which to camp for the night. We had intended to stop in the cave, but could not do so without water. We found water in about half a mile, and making up a large log-heap fire, we cooked our evening meal—that is, we cooked our meat by frying it stuck on the end of a stick…

Supper over, we wrapped our blankets around us, and threw ourselves on the ground before the fire to sleep.

"How clear and beautiful the stars look to night," said I.

"Yes," answered Jack, "but how cold and distant."

A Week in the Great Smoky Mountains (1860)

Monday, Nov. 7th—Up early and mending our fire, we discussed our frugal meal…To-day we mean to go to the top of Quonacatoosa, the highest peak of the Smoky, and to get back to Mr. Huskey's by night—a distance, in all, of sixteen miles. So we started. After going about three or four miles, we crossed the path by which we would return to Mr. H.'s, and there left all of our baggage, taking with us nothing but a piece of bread and meat for our dinner.

Within two miles of the top of the gap through which the path leading to North Carolina goes, we came upon five most beautiful falls or cascades, made by the headwaters of the Pigeon, tumbling over the cliffs. Jack informing me they had no name, I determined to christen them, telling Jack their names, so that he might inform future visitors, which he most religiously promised to do. [R. named each of the five waterfalls after young ladies of his acquaintance.]…*It would be difficult to decide which is the most beautiful of these charming cascades. Just by the "Ella Falls" is an overhanging rock, under which a young man from South Carolina, of the name of Psatter, lost his life by freezing to death. He endeavored to cross the mountains against the urgent remonstration of the people at Mr. Huskey's, who told him a snow storm was coming on. The storm came, and to protect himself from it, he crawled under that rock. A week after, he was found sitting there dead with both eyes pecked out by the birds. The hunters dug a grave for him where they found him, and there buried him*—requiescat in pace.

12

NOTES ON THE GEOGRAPHY OF THE MOUNTAIN DISTRICT OF WESTERN NORTH CAROLINA (1863)

Arnold Guyot

Geologist, geographer and explorer Arnold Henry Guyot (1807–1884) was born in Boudevilliers, Switzerland. After graduating from the College of Neuchatel in that country, Guyot elected to pursue a doctoral degree in natural sciences. Following five years of study of physics, chemistry and geology and the completion of his thesis, he was awarded a PhD in 1835 by the University of Berlin.

Guyot made excursions into the Alps to study glaciers, especially to test the theory that a significant portion of Europe had experienced an ice age. In 1838, he reported his discoveries concerning glacial formation, structure and movement in a paper presented to the Geological Society of France.

To escape political turmoil in Switzerland, Guyot immigrated to America in 1848, and the following year gave the prestigious Lowell Institute Lectures in Boston. Their publication that same year as *The Earth and Man*—which sought to explain the relationship between people's physical environment and their social, political and moral development—elevated him to one of America's most respected geographers.

Guyot moved to Princeton University in 1854 to accept a chair in physical geography and geology, which he occupied for the next thirty years. He measured the heights of peaks from Maine to South Carolina and devised topographic maps of them.

An entry by Gary Scott Smith in *American National Biography Online* concluded with these observations:

> *Guyot's investigations, maps, tables, textbooks, and articles significantly influenced the development of both American and international geography during the second half of the nineteenth century. His research and publications provided important data about many geological formations and stimulated other geographers to do their own fieldwork. His extensive meteorological observations contributed to the establishment in 1870 of the U.S. Weather Bureau (now the National Weather Bureau). A generous, energetic, devoutly religious man who enjoyed many close friendships, Guyot hiked and climbed mountains to obtain scientific information well beyond his seventieth birthday. He died in Princeton.*

In the Smokies.

Paul Fink and Myron H. Avery were two of the foremost explorers of the southern Appalachians—especially the Great Smoky Mountains—during the first half of the twentieth century. In a paper they coauthored for *Appalachia* magazine in 1936, Fink and Avery concluded,

> *Arnold Guyot was, beyond question, the most thorough explorer who ever penetrated the Appalachian system. Prior to the Civil War, he had traversed it throughout its northern terminus in New England to the southern end of the Blue Ridge in Georgia. Thus Guyot acquired an extensive knowledge of the Appalachian Mountains, such as has never been possessed by any other person and under conditions which can never again be duplicated. Guyot's objective was to record the elevation of the various peaks of this range, and to develop a general, systematic geographic outline of the mountain systems of the eastern United States.*

Guyot's delineations of his explorations of the northern Appalachians were published in various sources. But his explorations of the southern Appalachians, which took place from 1856 to 1860, were never published. Fortunately, they were preserved in a manuscript titled "Notes on the Geography of the Mountain District of Western North Carolina," which on February 22, 1863, he forwarded to the offices of the Coast and Geodetic Survey.

This so-called "Guyot Manuscript" remained buried in official archives until 1929. It was not published in full until 1938, when Myron H. Avery and Kenneth S. Boardman's "Arnold Guyot's Notes on the Geography of the Mountainous District of Western North Carolina" appeared in the *North Carolina Historical Review*. Of particular interest are his descriptions of the Great Smokies, the massive range that was, for the most part, placed into federal protection when the Great Smoky Mountains National Park was founded in 1934. I have indicated present-day measurements and place names as cited in William S. Powell's *The North Carolina Gazetteer* (1968).

> *To the South-west of the gorges through which the Big Pigeon* [Pigeon River] *escapes from the mountains, the chain rises rapidly in high pointed peaks and sharp ridges up to Luftee Knob 6,220* [6,216 feet]. *This is the beginning of the Smoky Mt. Chain proper, which by general elevation of both its peaks and its crest, by its perfect continuity, its great roughness and difficulty of approach, may be called the master chain of the Appalachian System.*
>
> *For over 50 miles it forms a high and almost impervious barrier between Tennessee and the inside basins of North Carolina. Only one tolerable road, or difficult mule path, in this whole distance if found to cross from the Great Valley of Tennessee into the interior basins of North Carolina…and the road reaches its summit, Road Gap* [Indian Gap] *as it is called, at an elevation of not less than 5,271 feet* [5,317 feet]. *It connects Sevierville, Tenn., with Webster, Jackson County, North Carolina, through the vallies of Little Pigeon and Ocona Luftee, the last of which is the main Northern tributary of the Tuckasegee.*
>
> *Between the gorges of the Big Pigeon and the Road Gap the top of these ridges are usually sharp and rocky, deeply indented, and winding considerably, covered with a dense growth of laurel and high trees, which makes travel over them extremely difficult and almost impractical. Neither the White Man nor the Indian hunter venture in the wilderness.*
>
> *Beyond the Road Gap, the chain of the Smoky Mts. rises still higher, but the top of the ridge ceases to be so rugged and sharp and will allow an easy path. One has been cut for my visit by order of Mr. Clingman* [Senator Thomas L. Clingman of North Carolina] *from the Road Gap to the highest peak. About six miles South-west of the Gap is the culminating point of the Smoky Mts., Smoky Dome or Clingman's Mt., 6,660 ft.* [Clingmans Dome, 6,642 feet] *which is thus only some 50 feet lower than the highest summit of the Black Mts.*
>
> *From this point the chain gradually descends. The black verdure of the Balsam Firs which elsewhere crown the highest summits, gives way to the green foliage of the Beeches and Oaks. After a short turn to the west it sends a long and powerful ridge called the Forney Ridge to the South-west, to the Little Tennessee. From the head of*

the Forney Ridge, the Big Stone Mt. 5,614 ft. [Silers Bald, 5,620 feet] *the main chain continues nearly due west, then curving gradually to the southwest terminates near the deep cut of the Tennessee* [Little Tennessee River] *in the Great Bald 4,922 feet* [Gregory Bald, 4,948 feet]—*All this portion of the Smoky Mts., from Forney Ridge is used by the Tennesseeans for grazing cattle. Numerous paths, therefore, run up the Western slopes, and along the dividing ridge. But the Eastern slope is still a wilderness, little frequented.*

Here the Little Tennessee cuts that high chain by a deep winding chasm, in which no room is left for a road on its immediate banks, the mountains nearby rising to 3,000 feet above it, and upwards; the point where it leaves the mountains being scarcely 900 ft. above the level of the sea.

13

A THOUSAND-MILE WALK
TO THE GULF (1867)

John Muir

Some of America's finest explorers and naturalists have made their way into the mountains of Western North Carolina. These number botanists such as William Bartram, André Michaux, John Fraser, John Lyon, Asa Gray and Charles Sprague Sargent; geologists Arnold Guyot and Arthur Keith; ornithologist William Brewster; and twentieth-century writers such as Horace Kephart, Donald Culross Peattie, Roger Tory Peterson and Edwin Way Teale. But none of these—with the possible exceptions of Bartram and Peterson—can rival John Muir's name recognition. As the founder and first president of the Sierra Club, he was without doubt this country's most influential conservationist.

Muir (1838–1914) was born in Dunbar, Scotland, the son of Daniel Muir, a farmer. The family migrated to a homestead near Portage, Wisconsin, in the late 1840s. Muir Sr. is reputed to have been a harsh disciplinarian who worked his family from dawn to dusk. But in his free time, his son became a keen observer of the natural world.

In 1860, Muir entered the University of Wisconsin, where he made excellent grades; nevertheless, after three years, he left Madison to travel through the Northern United States and Canada, thereby increasing his knowledge of the natural world, especially of plants. Then, in 1867, while working at a carriage parts shop, he suffered a blinding eye injury that changed the course of his life.

After miraculously regaining his sight, the rejuvenated young man resolved to turn his attention fulltime to the "University of the Wilderness." Already an accomplished long-distance walker, on September 1, 1867, Muir initiated years of wanderlust with a little stroll from Indianapolis, Indiana, where he was then residing, to Cedar Key, Florida. Traveling light, he carried a small bag that contained a comb, brush, towel, soap, a change of underclothing, a copy of Robert Burns's poems, Milton's *Paradise Lost*, a copy of the *New Testament* and a notebook, in which he made daily observations and rough pencil sketches of plants and animals. Written on the inside cover of the notebook are the words: "John Muir, Earth-planet, Universe"—his address for the remainder of his life.

The following year, Muir went to California, heading directly from San Francisco to the Sierra Nevada, on foot. He fell in love with the Sierras and was entranced by

American Holly.

Yosemite Valley. Accordingly, he campaigned for the establishment of Yosemite National Park, which became a reality in 1890, and two years later he organized the Sierra Club to foster conservation of wild lands. Muir served as the club's president until his death. During the years 1896 and1897, his influence with President Grover Cleveland helped establish thirteen forest reserves—which evolved into today's national forests. Along with

President Theodore Roosevelt, who became a close friend after camping with him in Yosemite in 1903, Muir fostered the designation of additional national forests, national monuments such as Muir Woods and national parks such as Sequoia.

His first book, *The Mountains of California*, was published in 1894. It was followed in his lifetime by others such as *Our National Parks* (1901), *Stickeen* (1909), *My First Summer in the Sierra* (1911) and *The Yosemite* (1912). *Travels in Alaska* (1915), *The Cruise of the Corwin* (1917) and *Steep Trails* (1918) appeared posthumously.

The nature notebook Muir kept during his 1867 walk, ably edited and with an important introduction by William Frederic Bade, was published by Houghton Mifflin Company in 1916 as *A Thousand-Mile Walk to the Gulf*. Bade titled the second chapter of the book "The Cumberland Mountains." Therein, one finds Muir's all too brief account of his crossing of the far southwestern tip of North Carolina.

"Mr. Beale"—the sheriff Muir encountered in Cherokee County—was William Beale. Margaret Walker Freel, in *Our Heritage: The People of Cherokee County, North Carolina, 1540–1955* (1956), described him as a native of Yorkshire, England, who had attended Oxford University before moving with his family to Murphy in 1855. He served as Cherokee County's sheriff during the Civil War and for some time afterward, even though "there was feeling that he was in sympathy with the North, and at times he had to go to the mountains for safety." He was also a schoolteacher, storekeeper, mineralogist and surveyor, "who had the first transit ever brought to the county," as well as "the first wagon with manufactured wheels and the first lamp which burned kerosene oil." Such was the background of the local man who befriended John Muir in September 1867, during his long walk from Indianapolis to Cedar Key.

> September 18. *Up the mountain on the state line. The scenery is far grander than any I ever before beheld. The view extends from the Cumberland Mountains on the north far into Georgia and North Carolina to the south, an area of about five thousand square miles. Such an ocean of wooded, waving, swelling mountain beauty and grandeur is not to be described. Countless forest-clad hills, side by side in rows and groups, seemed to be enjoying the rich sunshine and remaining motionless only because they were so eagerly absorbing it. All were united by curves and slopes of inimitable softness and beauty. Oh, these forest gardens of our Father! What perfection, what divinity, in their architecture! What simplicity and mysterious complexity of detail! Who shall read the teaching of these sylvan pages, the glad brotherhood of rills that sing in the valleys, and all the happy creatures that dwell in them under the tender keeping of a Father's care?*

> September 19. *Received another solemn warning of dangers on my way through the mountains. Was told by my worthy entertainer of a wondrous gap in the mountains which he advised me to see. "It is called Track Gap* [now Track Rock Gap State Archaeological Area in north Georgia],*" said he, "from the great number of tracks in the rocks—bird tracks, bar tracks, hoss tracks, men tracks, all in the solid rock as if it had been mud." Bidding farewell to my worthy mountaineer and all his comfortable wonders, I pursued my way to the South.*

As I was leaving, he repeated the warnings of danger ahead, saying that there were a good many people living like wild beasts on whatever they could steal, and that murders were sometimes committed for four or five dollars, and even less. While stopping with him I noticed that a man came regularly after dark to the house for his supper. He was armed with a gun, a pistol, and a long knife. My host told me that this man was at feud with one of his neighbors, and that they were prepared to shoot one another at sight. That neither of them could do any regular work or sleep in the same place two nights in succession. That they visited houses only for food, and as soon as the one that I saw had got his supper he went out and slept in the woods, without of course making a fire. His enemy did the same.

My entertainer told me that he was trying to make peace between these two men, because they both were good men, and if they would agree to stop their quarrel, they could then both go to work. Most of the food in this house was coffee without sugar, corn bread, and sometimes bacon. But the coffee was the greatest luxury which these people knew. The only way of obtaining it was by selling skins, or, in particular, "sang," that is ginseng, which found a market in far-off China.

My path all to-day led me along the leafy banks of the Hiwassee, a most impressive mountain river. Its channel is very rough, as it crosses the edges of upturned rock strata, some of them standing at right angles, or glancing off obliquely to right and left. Thus a multitude of short, resounding cataracts are produced, and the river is restrained from the headlong speed due to its volume and the inclination of its bed.

All the larger streams of uncultivated countries are mysteriously charming and beautiful, whether flowing in mountains or through swamps and plains. Their channels are interestingly sculptured, far more so than the grandest architectural works of man. The finest of the forests are usually found along their banks, and in the multitude of falls and rapids the wilderness finds a voice. Such a river is the Hiwassee, with its surface broken to a thousand sparkling gems, and its forest walls vine-draped and flowery as Eden. And how fine the songs it sings!

In Murphy I was hailed by the sheriff who could not determine by my colors and rigging to what country or craft I belonged. Since the war, every other stranger in these lonely parts is supposed to be a criminal, and all are objects of curiosity or apprehensive concern. After a few minutes' conversation with this chief man of Murphy I was pronounced harmless, and invited to his house, where for the first time since leaving home I found a house decked with flowers and vines, clean within and without, and stamped with the comforts of culture and refinement in all its arrangements. Striking contrast to the uncouth transitionist establishments from the wigwams of savages to the clumsy but clean log castle of the thrifty pioneer.

September 20. *All day among the groves and gorges of Murphy with Mr. Beale. Was shown the site of Camp Butler where General Scott had his headquarters when he removed the Cherokee Indians* [in 1838] *to a new home in the West. Found a number of rare and strange plants on the rocky banks of the river Hiwassee. In the afternoon, from the summit of a commanding ridge, I obtained a magnificent view of blue, softly curved mountain scenery. Among the trees I saw* Ilex [holly] *for the first time.*

14

THE GRANDFATHER OF
NORTH CAROLINA (1873)

Jehu Lewis

Except for a few reminiscences in this selection that suggest Jehu Lewis spent some of his early years in New England, nothing else is known about him. The *Lakeside Monthly* in which it appeared in 1873 was published in Chicago, Illinois.

As Kevin O'Donnell and Helen Hollingsworth noted in *Seekers of Scenery: Travel Writing from Southern Appalachia, 1840–1900* (2004), "Lewis traveled on foot, off-trail, at a time when recreational hiking was not yet popular in America. Rather than describing culture and local characters, in the mode of much of the writing of the time, Lewis writes here, instead, of flora, fauna, and topography."

In his opening paragraphs, the author made it clear that one of his purposes was to call the attention of readers in the American heartland to Western North Carolina—especially to Grandfather Mountain—where they might also enjoy the pleasures of mountain scenery, botanical exploration and high adventure.

> *The Western North Carolina Railroad traverses some of the finest scenery east of Yo Semite, starting from old Salisbury, which is an easy connection with all main lines of travel in the country…*
>
> *Fifty miles or less northerly from Salisbury…is Hickory Tavern. Here you may be so interested as to stay in the neighborhood for the season. But if you travel another northwesterly twenty miles, to the quiet old town of Lenoir, the seat of Caldwell county, when about half way, a bold summit, overtopping the surrounding mountains, dim in its thirty miles distance, but distinct and unmistakable in its lofty and striking outlines, will loom up before you.*
>
> *If the mountain tops be cloudless you will see a gigantic silhouette, as of an old, old man, with wrinkled brow, drooping nose, and sunken mouth, lying calm and still, as though stretched on his bier, his dead, stony face cutting sharply against the tender blue of the sky. Hence the mountain's name. And from the moment you first trace the lines of the wonderful profile, the GRANDFATHER becomes a reality catching the eye, and even the heart, with its majesty and touched with pathos…*

Scaling Grandfather Mountain.

You begin to long for a closer acquaintance, for an opportunity to penetrate the mysteries of that blue distance, and for a moment to stand on that far height and look down upon all the green-topped hills and wooded, billowy mountains, to the utmost horizon. Then, too, all through these mountains grow rare and beautiful plants: such lovely forms of fern, club-moss, moss and lichen, that, if you are a botanist—especially one in his first unassisted steps—you will look forward eagerly to the starting on the wild tramp over the hills and through the tangled forests to the path which loses itself upon the rugged sides of the Grandfather...

All summer long my home had been a farm-house in Lower Creek Valley, a few miles southwest of Lenoir…Provided with a haversack of food and a portable press for botanical specimens, I set out on the last morning of August…

The day was so far spent that I could not climb to the summit of the Grandfather and return before night, though the rocky mass frowned down upon me, apparently but half hour's walk distance. So I thankfully accepted a blanket and a place at Bill Estee's camp-fire, for the evening was cool and gave promise of frost.

In the crisp frosty air and paling starlight of early morning I was astir, hoping to gain the summit in time to see the sun rise. For a mile, a good road, cut through a dense growth of trees and rhododendrons, led up a winding ascent to an open field, from whence I looked forward and around, and perceived that I stood upon the throat of the Grandfather, while the chin towered, bold and rugged, above the forest before me…

Half unconsciously, I had followed the trail till it became dim and dimmer, and at last disappeared. I had now to depend upon instinct and careful observation to guide me, for the mountain-top was hidden from view by the dense growth of trees. Marking well my way, I went on, breaking here a bush, blazing there a small tree with my knife, scattering sprigs of laurel with the white under surface of the leaves upward—anything by which I might retrace my steps…

An open space, a glimpse of the summit, and a formidable-looking blackberry thicket confronted me, apparently girdling the mountain. Having learned to fear the terrible sharp claws of the Carolina blackberry, I hesitated and drew back; but seeing no alternative except to retreat, and not being ready for that, I boldly attacked the barrier. To my great surprise I found the canes almost thornless. I could even part them with my hands, and receive no hurt. [The blackberry species, *Rubus canadensis*, found in clearings in the higher elevations of the Blue Ridge, is essentially without prickles.]

After the briers, came a belt of black spruce [red spruce, *Picea rubens*] *and balsam firs* [Fraser fir, *Abies fraseri*], *with striped maple, mountain ash, and other trees shrubs of northern growth. These bushes, huge, sloping fragments of rock, and a rugged cliff, rose abruptly before me. Hurrah! That must be the summit! Climbing eagerly up the bare, rough rock, lo! It was only a jutting prominence on the mountain side, while beyond was a fearfully rugged, tangled wilderness of rocks and bushes; a huge pyramidal mass rose half a thousand feet above me…*

Climbing huge fragments of rock, only to swing myself down on the other side, by clinging to boughs of trees; creeping under arched passages and overhanging ledges; crawling on all-fours through thickets of laurel, so dense I cold not see the sky above me; and again clambering over the tops of bushes, so closely matted as to bear me entirely up from the ground; I became so fascinated with my success in mastering such difficulties, as to several times forget to mark the way. Then I would have to retrace my steps and bring up the clue.

I met with frequent indications that bears abound in these mountains; and once, in crawling through the laurels, placed my hand side by side with the fresh impress of a great heavy foot. It could not have been many hours since Bruin trod the same path I was following; but so long as he did not return to dispute my passage, the way would serve us both…

Ascending rapidly, I soon emerged upon a steep bare rock, with scarcely enough roughness of surface to afford footing. Cautiously climbing upward, hands lending aid to my feet, a little level spot was at length attained, in a sunny nook within twenty or thirty feet of the top…

Passing a rocky wall, I stood upon the brink of a precipice, which went down so steep I almost fancied I could cast a stone to the middle of the valley which skirts the mountain on the north; the depth so great that the trees, dwarfed by the distance, seemed almost like mosses at the bottom.

The only living thing in sight was a solitary hawk, poised on outspread wings, hanging motionless for a moment over the abyss, and then sailing swiftly and noiselessly away.

Not a sound came from those far depths; not a cloud marred the spotlessness of the crystalline sky; not a breeze swayed the bushes growing from the rifts of the rocks; all was still as the grave. I looked round and saw, on every side, the marks of violence and storm, and wondered at the udder calm.

A good, firm, easy way I found to mount the last remaining rock, the coping of the pyramid. But behold! It was not a pyramid at all. It was the projecting chin bone of the Grandfather!

To the northwest I could trace the elevations and depressions which fill out the whole profile. The nose about a mile, and the brow almost two miles distant, appeared to be near a hundred feet higher than the chin. Leaning upon the sharp crest, long I stood to gaze around the vast panorama spread out below me. Bounding the prospect in the far southwest, I could see the towering summits of the Black; while all around, like green, tossing billows, lay the wooded mountains, an expanse of almost unbroken forest from highest crests to deepest valleys.

The narrow, fertile valley of the Catawba, with its cultivated lands, and the broad upland farms of Burke county showed faintly under the golden haze…while far away toward Tennessee, were to be seen several farms upon the mountain tops; a few smaller clearings here and there in the valleys or on the sides of the mountains; but aside from these, the appearance was that of a wild, uninhabitable country.

One long, lingering gaze upon the landscape of grandeur: one reluctant, sad, and final adieu, and bending my eyes upon the traced pathway, I began the descent.

15

THE GREAT SOUTH (1875)

Edward King

Journalist, novelist and travel writer Edward King (1848–1896) was born in Middlefield, Massachusetts. King's career in journalism began in 1864, when he left home to become a reporter for the *Springfield (Massachusetts) Daily Union*. In 1870, he went over to the *Boston Morning Journal*. His first major assignment was as a correspondent during the Franco-Prussian War. King enthusiastically thrust himself into the thick of the conflict, assisting with the wounded and twice getting arrested by the Germans as a spy. His closely observed and carefully reported newspaper and magazine work quickly earned him the reputation of being "one of the ablest of the younger American journalists."

In the early 1870s, King was bankrolled by *Scribner's Monthly* to the tune of $30,000 to travel throughout the South via train, riverboat, coastal steamer, wagon, horseback, stagecoach and on foot. His magazine articles were subsequently collected and published in 1875 as *The Great South: A Record of Journeys in Louisiana, Texas, the Indian Territory, Missouri, Arkansas, Mississippi, Alabama, Georgia, Florida, South Carolina, North Carolina, Kentucky, Tennessee, Virginia, West Virginia, and Maryland*. The book was published simultaneously in England as *The Southern States of North America*.

In their 1973 introduction to the Louisiana State University Press reissue of *The Great South*, the editors quoted southern historian Fletcher M. Green, who was of the opinion that King's book represented the "fullest and at the same time one of the most accurate and revealing" of the postbellum travel accounts.

King's travel party, which varied in number throughout the trip, entered Western North Carolina from east Tennessee in the spring of that year. In 1873, they crossed Mount Sterling (in the present Great Smoky Mountains National Park in Haywood County) and visited "Bennett's" in "Catalouche" (present Cataloochee Valley in the national park near Waynesville). Traversing Jonathan's Creek, they went to Waynesville. After crossing the Balsams, they visited Webster and Franklin, and then proceeded up the Cullasaja River to Whiteside Mountain. They then descended the Tuckasegee River to present Cullowhee, where Western Carolina University is now located. The last leg

Whiteside Mountain.

of their journey in Western North Carolina was from Asheville to Mount Mitchell, and then along the upper French Broad into South Carolina.

In the following selection, King described his visit to Whiteside Mountain, situated about three and a half miles northeast of present Highlands. They spent several nights at "Wright's," the residence of James Wright, who had moved to the base of Short Off Mountain in 1865. The log cabin served as a boardinghouse for the few visitors to the Highlands Plateau in those days.

Now situated on U.S. Forest Service lands and smaller private holdings, Whiteside Mountain is a popular tourist destination accessed by a side road and foot trails from U.S. 64. Whiteside Mountain rises 2,100 feet in dramatic relief to reach an elevation of 4,930 feet at its summit. Sheer rock walls, rising vertically 400 to 700 feet, create the rock faces on three sides of the mountain.

> *The shadows were creeping over the mighty hills as we hastened back across the wooded slopes, and leaving the main road a little farther on, entered a narrow trail, obstructed by swampy holes and gnarled tree-roots. Three miles brought us to "Wright's"—the little farm-house in a deadening from which we obtained a view of Short-Off—and the forest which hid the approaches to "Whiteside"…*

At dawn of next day we plunged into the woods beyond Wright's, and wound through a trail whose trace we of the cities should soon have lost, but in which our companions of the neighborhood easily kept until we reached a wooded hill-side, whence we could see the Devil's Court-House, and catch a glimpse of Whiteside's top.

The former is a grand, rocky bluff, with its foot planted among the thickets, and its brow crowned with a rugged castle-like formation. The ragged sides are here and there stained like the walls of an old building, and it is not difficult to imagine that one is beholding the ruined walls of some giant castle. The Surveyor urged us forward, and our stout horses soon brought us to the clearing, where we were compelled to leave them, and climb the remaining distance on foot.

Here, more than 4,000 feet above the ocean-level, the sun beat down with extreme fierceness, and was reflected back from the hard white of the rocks with painful intensity. The horses tethered, the Judge sprang up the narrow pathway, and regardless of rattlesnakes, we clambered on all fours, clinging sometimes to roots, sometimes to frail and yielding bunches of grass and ferns; now trod breathlessly a path in the black dirt on the edge of a rock sixty feet high; now hung, poised by our hands, from one ledge while we swung to another; and now dug out footholds in the stone when we ascended an almost perpendicular wall.

Finally we came to a plateau covered with a kind of gorse, and with laurel bushes scattered here and there; pushing through this, we wound, by a gradual ascent, to the summit of Whiteside, and the edge of the precipice. There we were face to face with the demon of the abyss. Let me tell you how the Surveyor saw him.

"One day," said the Surveyor, seating himself with admirable carelessness on the dreadful slope of a rock overhanging the awful depths, "I was taking some levels below, and at last thought I would climb Whiteside. While I was coming up a storm passed over the mountains, and when I reached the top everything was hidden in such a dense mist, fog, or cloud, that one could hardly see his hand before his face. I strolled on until I reached a spot which I thought I recognized, and sat down, stretching my feet carelessly.

"Luckily enough, I didn't move; I was mighty still, for I was tired, and the fog was solemn-like; but pretty soon it blew away right smart, and dog my skin if I wasn't perched on the very outer edge of this line of rock, and about two inches between me and twelve hundred feet of sheer fall.

"I saw the trees in Cashier's valley, and the clearings, and then the sky, for I didn't look twice at the fall below me; but I flattened myself against the rock, and turned over; and I never want to come up here in a fog again."

Imagine a waterfall 2,000 feet high suddenly turned to stone, and you have the general effect of the Whiteside precipice as seen in the single, terrified, reluctant glance which you give from the top. There is the curve and the grand, dizzy bend downward; were it not for occasional clumps of foliage down the sides, the resemblance would be absolute.

The mountain itself lies rooted in the western slope of the Blue Ridge. The veteran [Silas] McDowell has compared it to the carcass of some great monster, upon whose head you climb, and along whose mammoth spine you wander, giddy with terror each time you gaze over the skeleton sides.

The main rock stands on a hill 1,600 feet high, and its upper crest is 2,400 feet above the branch of the Chattooga river, which runs near the hill's base. From top to tail of the mammoth skeleton the distance is 800 feet. Viewed at a proper distance, in the valley below, from its south-east front, it is one of the sublimest natural monuments in the United States. The sunshine plays upon walls which are at times of dazzling whiteness, and the sheer fall seems to continue to the very level of the valley, although it is here and there broken by landings.

But the outlook! It was the culmination—the finishing stroke of all our rich and varied mountain surprises! When we were seated on the white crag, over which a fresh breeze perpetually blew, the "wrinkled" world beneath us literally "crawled." Everything seemed dwarfed and insignificant below. Even the brother crags—to the south-west, Fodderstack and Black Rock, and Stooly, to the north-west—although in reality rising nearly to the elevation of Whiteside, seemed like small hills.

To the north-east, as far as the eye could reach, rose a multitude of sharply defined blue and purple peaks, the valleys between them, vast and filled with frightful ravines, seeming the merest gullies on the earth's surface. Farther off than this line of peaks rose the dim outlines of the Balsam and Smoky ranges. In the distant south-west, looking across into Georgia, we could descry Mount Yonah [also called Yunah Mountain], lonely and superb, with a cloud-wreath about his brow; sixty miles away, in South Carolina, a flash of sunlight revealed the roofs of the little German settlement of Walhalla; and on the south-east, beyond the precipices and ragged projections, towered up Chimney Top mountain, while the Hog Back bent its ugly form against the sky, and Cold mountain rose on the left. Turning to the north, we beheld Yellow mountain, with its square sides, and Short-Off. Beyond and beyond, peaks and peaks, and ravines and ravines! It was like looking down on the world from a balloon...

There is one pass on Whiteside which, though eminently dangerous, is now and then essayed, and Jonas and one of the woodmen of our party resolved to try it. While we commoner mortals drank in the wonderful view, and hobnobbed with the clouds, these adventurers climbed down the precipice's sides, and coming to a point not far from the Devil's Court-House, where the pass begins, launched themselves boldly forward. To gain a cave which is supposed in former times to have been the abode of an Indian sorcerer or medicine man, they were compelled to step out upon a narrow ledge running along the very side of the cliff, turning a corner with no support above or below. The ledge or path is, at its beginning, two feet wide, and as it nears the cavern, not more than eighteen inches in width. A single misstep or a failing of the nerves would have precipitated them a thousand feet into the valley, and above them the comfortless rock rose 300 feet. Hugging the wall, and fairly flattening themselves against it, they calmly went forward and reached the cavern in safety. Returning, with their eyes blinded by the shadows of the rocky crevice, the demon of the abyss seized upon Jonas, and prompted him to look down. One glance, and the awful depths seemed to claim him. He shrank toward the wall, dug his fingernails into the crevices, uttered a faint cry, looked up, and was saved.

16

THE MOUNTAIN REGION OF
NORTH CAROLINA (1877)

Christian Reid

Frances Christine Fisher Tiernan (1846–1920), the author who wrote under the pseudonym "Christian Reid," was born in Salisbury, North Carolina. After the early death of her mother and the loss of her father during the Civil War, Fisher and her brother and sister were left in the care of Christine Fisher, their aunt. Frances was, for the most part, educated at home by her aunt. In 1887, she married James Marquis Tiernan, a mineralogist and agent of the North Pacific Railroad.

When Fisher decided to write for a living before publishing her first full-length novel, *Valerie Aylmer*, in 1870, she chose to protect her privacy with the pseudonym "Christian" because of its ambiguity regarding sex and "Reid" because it seemed modest and unassuming. During a long career, she wrote forty-two novels, four novelettes, numerous short stories and poems, a drama and several travel sketches.

Tiernan's descriptive powers—her greatest strength as a writer—were accentuated in her travel sketches. Her semi-fictionalized travel account *The Land of the Sky* was published in 1876. It drew nationwide attention to Western North Carolina as "a vacationland of blue valleys, rippling streams, and awe-inspiring mountains," creating a phrase later used by the Southern Railway Company as its advertising slogan and still used by others to describe the area.

Thomas L. Clingman had written an article for *Appletons' Journal* in 1861 titled "Mount Pisgah, North Carolina" that was collected in his *Selections from the Speeches and Writings of Thomas L. Clingman* (1877). Therein, he provided one of the first comprehensive overviews written for the layman about the topography of the North Carolina mountains. Acknowledging that she utilized Clingman's concepts and text, Tiernan wrote for *Appletons' Journal* a lengthy travel article published in 1877 as "The Mountain Region of North Carolina." In places the article reads like a modern Chamber of Commerce brochure, but her overview of the vast and complex mountain ranges that make up Western North Carolina was carefully crafted.

> *It is safe to assert that there is no part of that vast extent of country, which lies between the St. Lawrence and the Gulf of Mexico, that is so slightly known, and so little*

Mount Pisgah.

appreciated as the mountain region of North Carolina. While the White Mountains and the Adirondacks are yearly thronged with tourists and the mountains of Virginia have been for half a century known to pleasure-seekers, these wild and beautiful highlands are to-day less visited, less written of, and less talked of, than the defiles of the Sierra Nevada and the peaks of the Rocky Mountains. Comparatively speaking, indeed, there are few persons who are even aware that the grandest scenery east of the Mississippi is to be found were they to enter a land where the great Appalachian system reaches its loftiest altitude, in North Carolina…

Let us take a glance at the map, to assist us in forming some idea of the extent of the region. We perceive that it is encircled by two great mountain chains—the Blue Ridge forming its eastern boundary, the Great Smoky the western—within which lies an elevated land, two hundred and fifty miles in length, with an average breadth of fifty miles. It is also traversed by cross-chains, that run directly across the country, and from which spurs of greater or lesser height lead off in all directions. Of these transverse ranges there are four—the Black, the Balsam, the Cullowhee [Cowee], and Nantahala. Between each lies a region of valleys, formed by the noble rivers and their minor tributaries, where a healthful atmosphere and picturesque surroundings are combined with a soil of singular fertility.

The Blue Ridge is the natural barrier dividing the waters falling into the Atlantic Ocean from those of the Mississippi Valley, and its bold and beautiful heights are better known than the grander steeps of the western chain. It abounds in scenery of the most romantic description. The streams that burst from the brows of the mountains leap down their sides in unnumbered flashing cascades, while cliffs and palisades of rock diversify the splendid sweep of towering peaks and lofty pinnacles…

On the western side of this "land of the sky" runs the chain of the Great Smoky— comprising the groups of the Iron, the Unaka, and the Roan Mountains—which, from its massiveness of form and general elevation, is the master-chain of the whole Alleghany range. Though its highest summits are a few feet lower than the peaks of the Black Mountain, it presents a continuous series of high peaks which nearly approach that altitude—its culminating point, Clingman's Dome, rising to the height of six thousand six hundred and sixty feet [6,642 feet]. Though its magnitude is much greater than that of the Blue Ridge, this range is cut at various points by the mountain-rivers, which with resistless impetuosity tear their way through the heart of its superb heights in gorges of terrific grandeur…

The most famous of the transverse ranges is that of the Black Mountain, the dominating peak of which is now well known to be the loftiest of the Atlantic summits. One is surprised to consider how long the exact height of these mountains remained undetermined, and Mount Washington, in New Hampshire, was esteemed the highest point east of the Rocky Mountains, while, in truth, not fewer than thirty peaks in North Carolina surpass it in altitude. The Black Mountain is a group of colossal heights, which attain their greatest elevation near the Blue Ridge. With its two great branches, it is more than twenty miles long, and its rugged sides are covered with a wilderness of almost inaccessible forest…A great deal can be seen in even one visit to the summit of Mount Mitchell; and, although nothing is more uncertain than the weather of the Black, if the visitor is fortunate enough to find a clear day, he will obtain a view which is almost boundless in extent. All Western Carolina lies spread below him, together with portions of Virginia, Tennessee, Georgia, and South Carolina. He can trace across the breadth of the Old Dominion the long, undulating line of the Blue Ridge [escarpment], which, entering North Carolina, passes under the Black, and thence runs southerly until it reaches South Carolina…

Returning to the region west of the Blue Ridge, we find the Black diverging into two chains, one of which stretches northward, with a series of cone-like peaks rising along its dark crest, and ends in a majestic pyramid, while the northwestern ridge runs out toward the Smoky. Another branch is the range of Craggy, which trends southward, with its lofty peaks the Bull's Head, the Pinnacle, and the Dome in bold relief…

Northward of the Black Mountain stand two famous heights, which Professor Guyot calls, "the two great pillars on both sides of the North Gate to the high mountain-region of North Carolina." These are the Grandfather Mountain in the Blue Ridge, and the Roan Mountain in the Smoky. Both of these command a wide view, but the Roan is specially remarkable for the extent of territory which it overlooks…

Next to the Black, in the order of transverse chains, comes the Balsam, which, in point of length and general magnitude, is chief of the cross-ranges. It is fifty miles long, and its peaks average six thousand feet; while, like the Blue Ridge, it divides all waters, and is pierced by none. From its southern extremity two great spurs run out in a northerly direction. One terminates in the Cold Mountain, which is more than six thousand feet high; the other rises into the beautiful peak of Pisgah, one of the most noted landmarks of the country.

Among the mountains which, seen from Asheville, lie in blue waves against the southern horizon, this commanding pyramid stands forth most prominently, and from its symmetrical outline, not less than its eminence, attracts the eye at once. Nor does this attraction end with the first view. Its harmonious lines are a constant source of delight, and the robes of soft color which it wears are constantly changing and ever charming. To see it, as it often appears, a glorified crest of violet, against a sky divinely flushed with sunset rose and gold, is one of those pleasures which custom cannot stale.

It follows, naturally, with all who have the true spirit of mountaineering, that they desire to stand on that uplifted eminence. Those who carry this desire into effect are gratified by a view less extensive than that of the Black or the Balsam, but hardly less worth beholding. The summit of Mount Pisgah forms the corner of the counties of Buncombe, Henderson, Transylvania, and Haywood, and over the outspread face of each—broken by innumerable hill-waves and smiling valleys—the gaze passes to where the tall peaks send their greeting from the borders of South Carolina and Tennessee. Near by rise the Cold Mountain and Shining Rock, with the wooded heights of Haywood rolling downward to the fertile valley of the Pigeon—a beautiful stream, which finally cuts its way through the Smoky and joins the French Broad in Tennessee.

The course of the latter river is plainly to be marked by its width of cultivated lowlands, as it passes through Transylvania and Henderson, to where Asheville lies—surrounded by an amphitheatre of hills. Among these hills the river enters, and pours its current along a constantly deepening gorge, narrow as a Western canyon, and inexpressibly grand, until it also cuts a passage through the Smoky, and reaches Tennessee...A journey along this gorge is something which no lover of Nature should forego. I have known those who have not looked on its beauty for thirty or forty years, in whose memory still remain fresh as if they had been seen but yesterday—the great overhanging cliffs, the verdure-clad mountains, the giant boulders that strew the channel—tokens of Titanic warfare, round which the triumphant water whirls and surges in tossing rapids and the fairy islets which it holds in so gentle an embrace. Over the heights which hem this gorge Pisgah looks, and sees the distant mountains of Mitchell and Yancey mingling their forms and colors with the clouds...

It was the good fortune of the writer to be one of a party who made the ascent [of the Balsams] during the past summer, and it is little to say that all difficulties and perils were forgotten when we stood at last on the summit of the highest peaks, and felt that we were in the center of the great system of diverging heights spread around us, far as the gaze could reach, to the uttermost bounds of land and sky. There is an intense exhilaration of mind and body consequent upon attaining such an elevation, and we were exceedingly fortunate in having two days of perfect weather—days of the radiant softness which only September gives.*

*The spot where we found ourselves was a treeless tract of several hundred acres on top of the Balsam range [one of the numerous natural grassy balds found in the higher elevations of the southern mountains]. *The Cherokees believe that these open spaces are the footprints of the devil, made as he stepped from mountain to mountain, and this largest prairie they regard with peculiar awe as his favorite sleeping-place—probably selected because he likes now and then a complete change of climate. On maps of the State this point is marked "The Devil's Old Field," and, apart from the association with his satanic majesty, the title is not altogether inapposite. So peculiar is the appearance of these openings, where grass and bushes of all kinds flourish luxuriantly, that one is almost forced to believe that at some remote period man had his habitation here…*

Having been bold enough to pitch our camp in the midst of "The Devil's Old Field," we were probably punished by finding ourselves next morning wrapped in mist at the time that we should have been witnessing the sunrise beyond a thousand peaks. By eight o'clock, however, the clouds lifted, the mist dissolved away, and seated on the rocky crest of a high knob, with air so lucid and fresh that it seemed rather of heaven than earth fanning our brows, we were truly "girdled with the gleaming world." On one side spread the scenes over which we had journeyed—every height south of the Black clearly visible, and distinctly to be identified—while on the other the country on which we had come to gaze stretched westward, until its great ridges, like giant billows, blended their sapphire outlines with the sky. Overlooking this immense territory, one felt overwhelmed by its magnitude, and the imagination vainly strove to picture the innumerable scenes of loveliness that lay below, among what seemed a very chaos of peaks, gorges, cliffs, and vales.

17

THE HEART OF THE
ALLEGHANIES (1883)

Wilbur G. Zeigler and Ben S. Grosscup

Wilbur G. Zeigler (1857–1935) and Ben Grosscup (1858–1935) coauthored *The Heart of the Alleghanies or Western North Carolina: Comprising Its Topography, History, Resources, People, Narratives, Incidents, and Pictures of Travel, Adventures in Hunting and Fishing, and Legends of Its Wilderness* (1883). "Alleghanies" was used as an early designation for the southern Appalachians, including especially Western North Carolina, until about 1900.

Little had previously been known about the backgrounds of either of these authors or the role each played in the writing of their book. But recent research has uncovered additional information. (See the three anonymous citations and the Ellison-Murphree citation in Secondary Sources.)

Grosscup was born in Ashland, Ohio. He graduated from Wittenberg College in 1879 and was admitted to the Ohio Bar in 1884, after which he set up practice in his hometown. By 1890, he had moved to Tacoma, Washington, where he lived until 1918, before moving to Seattle. Grosscup was a partner in the law firm Grosscup & Morrow. In addition to serving as western counsel for the Northern Pacific Railway, he also served as president of the Washington State Bar Association (1912–18) and was a vice-president of the American Bar Association

Zeigler was born in Fremont, Ohio, the son of a prominent merchant. The family moved to Western North Carolina in 1878. In February 1879, he began submitting poems to the *North Carolina (Asheville) Citizen* newspaper with titles such as "One Midwinter Morning" and "The Suicide." In May of that year—by that time designated a "Special Correspondent" of the newspaper—he began contributing lengthy regional travel articles under headlines such as "On Foot Across the Mountains," "Trout Fishing in Cataluchee" and "A Bear Drive on the Balsams," which were revised and incorporated into *The Heart of the Alleghanies*.

Later in 1879, a note in the *Citizen*, headlined "Gone Back to Ohio," advised readers that Zeigler, along with his mother and father, "left last week for Sandusky, Ohio." He studied law in Cleveland, Ohio, was admitted to the Ohio bar in 1881 and joined the

Black Bear.

law firm of Buckland and Buckland in his hometown. A biographical note published in *The Bay of San Francisco* (1892) read:

> *After a year's practice as a member of this firm, Mr. Zeigler became interested in literary matters, and, with an associate, went South and devoted some time to the preparation of an illustrated descriptive and historical work, entitled The Heart of the Alleghanies; or, Western North Carolina…In 1883 Mr. Zeigler came to San Francisco and…is now in partnership with Philip G. Galpin, the firm being Galpin & Zeigler. Their business is very heavy, being entirely of a civil nature, particularly land, patent and probate practice.*

It's probable that Zeigler practiced law for the remainder of his professional life in the San Francisco area. He did write two other books: *It was Marlowe: A Story of the Secret of Three Centuries* (1895), a fictionalized account that sought to prove that Christopher Marlowe was the author of the plays attributed to Shakespeare; and *Story of the Earthquake and Fire: San Francisco* (1906).

In 1882, Zeigler had returned to Western North Carolina with Grosscup to accumulate additional travel accounts to supplement those previously written by Zeigler and to make a book. In doing so, they also utilized newspaper accounts written by others. The story of how Zeigler and Grosscup worked together during this literary venture was revealed in an anonymous biographical sketch of Zeigler (quite possibly written by Zeigler himself) that appeared in *The Builders of a Great City: San Francisco's Representative Men* (1891):

> *At this time the question of [Zeigler's] following an exclusive literary or legal career was demanding an answer. Several journeys to the picturesque mountains of Western North Carolina had been made by him while acting as a correspondent for Northern newspapers, and the favorable reception which his communications had met, as well as the success which had attended the publication of other literary productions written about this time, turned his mind toward literature. While in this frame of thought he determined to put the result of his travels and observations of life and nature in the Southern Mountains into book form. Ben. S. Grosscup, now an attorney-at-law in Ashland, O[hio], united with him in the plan, and together they paid a last visit to Western North Carolina...Mr. Grosscup, who had had some experience in statistical and biographical work, took up the treatment of the resources, history and Indian occupation. The other branches of the manifold subject were assumed by Mr. Zeigler, who, in order to fit himself for truthful representation of the country and people, traveled both on foot and horseback through the twenty mountainous counties of the region. He dragged an artist with him into the wilderness to sketch the scenery, hunted with the bearers of flint-lock rifles for adventures, mingled with every class of life for experiences, danced at hoe-downs, visited moonshiners' stills in lonely ravines, attended baptisms and shooting-matches, rode the circuits with the lawyers, and with the happy faculty of seeing the interesting and amusing sides of things, wrote enthusiastically of what he had seen, felt and heard.*

The Heart of the Alleghanies was published jointly in Raleigh and Cleveland in 1783, the same year that Zeigler moved to San Francisco to practice law. The book, 374 pages in length, consisted of an introduction, ten chapters, twenty-two illustrations and a map of Western North Carolina. The coauthors wrote in a lively fashion about the Cherokees and their lore; the native mountaineers and their lore; bear hunting and trout fishing; famous hunters and renowned fishermen; farming and livestock; mountain scenery and customs; the coming of tourism and mining; the distinctive characteristics of Asheville and other mountain communities; and much more. It would be difficult to think of a topic they didn't touch upon, often in passing but not infrequently in depth. The book is a neglected classic of southern Appalachian studies—one that deserves to be reprinted in a modern annotated edition.

This selection, probably written by Zeigler, is from the second chapter, "In the Haunts of the Black Bear." It described a midwinter bear hunt made with Wid

Medford—a famous nineteenth-century hunter and guide—and other Haywood County mountaineers.

> *The black bear, native to North America, still exists in large numbers on the wildest ranges of the southern mountains...Bruin's usual haunts are in those melancholy forests which hood the heads of the Black, Smoky, and Balsam ranges, and deck a few summits of the Blue Ridge, resorted to either from liking, or to avoid his enemies; and it is only when pushed by hunger or when his tooth has become depraved by a bait of hog, taken during one of these starving periods, that he appears on the lower slopes or in the cultivated valleys...*
>
> *With this slight introduction, the writer proposes to convey to the reader some idea of what bear hunting in the heart of the Alleghanies is like; what one must expect to encounter, and what sort of friends he is likely to make on such expeditions. Besides the usual equipments carried by every hunter, it would be well to take a rubber blanket and have the guide carry an ax.*
>
> *It was one night about the 1st of December that we were in camp; eight of us, huddled together under a low bark roof, and within three frail sides of like material. Around the camp lay seventeen dogs. The ground beneath us was cold and bare, except for a thin layer of ferns lately bundled in by some of the party. Before the front of the shelter lay a great fire of heavy logs, heaped close enough for a long-legged sleeper to stick his feet in, while his head rested on the bolster log. The hot flames, fanned by a strong wind, leaped high and struggled up into the darkness. On long sticks, several of the group were toasting chunks of fat pork; others were attending to black tin pails of water boiling for coffee, while the remaining few were eating lunches already prepared. The wood crackled, and occasionally the unseasoned chestnut timber snapped, sending out showers of sparks. Around and within the circle of firelight, stood the trees with stripped, gaunt limbs swaying in the wind. Above, clouds rolled darkly, concealing the face of the sky...*
>
> *Our encampment was on Old Bald; not the famous shaking mountain, but of the Balsams, eight miles south of Waynesville....Near where we encamped, and below on the Beech Flats, stand trees as stately and magnificent as any ever touched by woodman's ax. We noticed several cherries measuring four and a half feet through, and towering, straight as masts, 70 feet before shooting out a limb; poplars as erect and tall to their lower branches and of still greater diameter; chestnuts from 15 to 33 feet in circumference, and thousands of sound, lofty linns [basswoods], ashes, buckeyes, oaks, and sugar maples. A few hemlocks considerably exceed 100 feet in height...On the Beech Flats there is no underbrush, except where the rhododendron hedges the purling streams. In places the plain path, the stately trees, and the level or sloping ground, covered only with the mouldering leaves of autumn, form parks more magnificent than those kept in trim by other hands than nature's.*
>
> *The best hounds, known as the "leaders," were fastened to poles stuck in the ground at the corners of our lodge. This was done to prevent them starting off during the night on the trail of a wolf, raccoon, or wildcat, thereby exhausting themselves for the*

contemplated bear hunt. The rest of the pack were either standing around, looking absently into the fire, or had already stretched themselves out in close proximity to it.

"The way them curs crawl up to the blaze," said Wid Medford, "is a shore sign thet hits goin' ter be cold nuff ter snow afore mornin'."

Israel Medford, nicknamed Wid, the master-hunter of the Balsam range, is a singular character, and a good representative of the old class of mountaineers, who, reared in the wilderness, still spend most of their time in hunting and fishing. He possesses a standard type of common sense; an abundance of native wit…is a close observer, a perfect mimic, and a shrewd judge of character. His reputation as a talker is wide-spread; and, talking to the point, he commands the closest attention. His conversation abounds in similes; and, drawn as they are from his own observation, they are always striking. He is now sixty-five years old, and has been all his life a resident of Haywood county.

That night as he sat cross-legged close to the fire, turning in the flames a stick with a slice of fat pork on it, with his broad-brimmed hat thrown on the ground, fully exposing his thick, straight, gray locks, and clear, ruddy, hatchet-shaped face, bare but for a red mustache, lighted up with youthful animation, he kept shaking the index finger of his right hand, while in his talk he jumped from one subject to another with as much alacrity as his bow legs might carry him over the mountains…

We ascended Old Bald by a trail termed the "winds." It was icy underfoot, and some of the party had severe falls before we issued, from the dwarf beeches, upon the bare backbone of the range. Although no breeze was stirring that morning on the north side of the mountain, a bitter, winter blast was sweeping the summit. It cut through our clothing like wizard, sharp-edged knives that left no traces except the tingling skin. This blast had chased off every cloud, leaving clear, indigo-blue depths for the sun, just lifting over Cold Spring mountain, to ride through. As we reached the bare, culminating point of the narrow ridge between Old Bald and Lone Balsam, the sun had cleared himself from the mountain tops; and, red and round, doubly increased in size, he was shedding his splendor on a scene unsurpassed in beauty and wild sublimity. The night rain, turning to sleet on the summits of the mountains, had encased the black balsam forests, covering the Spruce Ridge and Great Divide, in armors of ice. They glistened like hills and pinnacles of silver in the sunlight. Below the edges of these iced forests, stood the deciduous trees of the mountains, brown and bare. No traces of the storm clung to them. The hemlocks along the head-prongs of the Richland were green and dark under the shadows of the steep declivities…The white houses of Waynesville were shining in the sunlight pouring through the gap towards the Pigeon…

As we descended into the low gap between Lone Balsam and the next pinnacle of the Balsams, Ickes, who had started in advance, came out in sight, on the ridge top, at a point some distance below us. Just at the moment he appeared, a turkey rose, like a buzzard, out of the winter grass near him, and was about to make good its flight for the iced forests beyond, when his gun came to his shoulder, a flash and a report succeeded, and the great bird whirled and fell straight downward into the firs. The mountaineers yelled with delight…A mountain turkey is no small game. This one was

89

*a magnificent specimen; a royal turkey-gobbler, that by stretching his brilliant neck
would have stood four feet high…*

*Although in December, a luxuriant greenness mantled everything, except where beds
of ferns had found root and then faded with the approach of autumn, or the yellow
leaves of the few scattered hard wood trees lay underfoot. The rich, black soil was well
grown with that species of grass that dies during the summer and springs up heavy and
green in the fall. Mosses, with stems and leaves like diminutive ferns, covered every ledge
of rock and crag, and formed for the trail a carpet soft and springy. This trail is as
crooked as a rail fence…It was hard enough to crawl up and down the moss-mantled
rocks and cliffs, and over or under an occasional giant balsam that, yellow with age,
had fallen from its own feebleness; but, along the narrow backbone approaching the
Great Divide, a recent hurricane had spread such devastation in its path as to render
walking many times more difficult.*

*For two miles, along this sharp ridge, nearly every other tree had been whirled by
the storm from its footing. They not only covered the path with their trunks bristling
with straight branches; but, instead of being cut off short, the wind had torn them up
by the roots, lifting thereby all the soil from the black rocks, and leaving great holes for
us to descend into, cross and then ascend. It was a continual crawl and climb for this
distance…*

*There were only three stands, and Wid and I, with the three dogs, occupied one
of these. It was a rather low dip in the ridge. We seated ourselves on a pile of rocks,
upholstered with mosses, making an easy and luxurious couch…A dense, black forest
surrounded us. Where the hollow reached the center-line of the ridge it sunk down on
the other side rather abruptly toward the Richland. This was the wildest front of the
mountain. At one point near the stand an observer can look down into what is called
the Gulfs. The name is appropriate. It is an abyss as black as night. Its depth is
fully 2,000, possibly 2,500 feet. No stream can be seen. It is one great, impenetrable
wilderness.*

*The trees began to drip as we sat there, and the air grew warm. With this warmth
a little life was awakened in the sober and melancholy forest. A few snow-birds
[juncos] twittered in the balsams; the malicious blue-jay screamed overhead, and
robins, now and then, flew through the open space. The most curious noise of these
forests is that of the boomer, a small red squirrel, native to the Alleghanies. He haunts
the hemlock-spruce, and the firs, and unlike the gray squirrel, the presence of man seems
to make him all the more noisy. Perched, at what he evidently deems a safe distance,
amid the lugubrious evergreen foliage of stately balsams, he sings away like the shuttle
of a sewing-machine. The unfamiliar traveler would insist that it was a bird thus
rendering vocal the forest.*

*Wid had been silent for several minutes. Suddenly he laid his hand softly on my
knee, and without saying a word pointed to the dogs. They lay at our feet, with ropes
round their necks held by the old hunter. Three noses were slightly elevated in the air,
and the folds of six long ears turned back…then as a slight breeze came to us from the
south, they jumped to their feet, as though electrified, and began whining.*

"Thar's suthin' in the wind," whispered Wid. "I reckon hits the music o' the pack. Sh_____! Listen!"

A minute passed, in which Wid kicked the dogs a dozen times to quiet them, and then we heard a faint bell-like tinkle. The likening of the baying of a pack of hounds to the tinkling of bells is as true in fact as it is beautiful in simile. There is every intonation of bells of all descriptions, changing with distance and location. It was a mellow, golden chiming at the beginning; then it grew stronger, stronger, until it swung through the air like the deep resonant tones of church bells. Did you ever hear it sweeping up a mountain side? It would light with animation the eyes of a man who had never pulled a trigger; but how about the hunter who hears it? He feels all the inspiration of the music, but mingled with it are thoughts of a practical nature, and a sportsman's kindling ardor to see the "varmint" that rings the bells. It steadily grew louder, coming with every echo right up the wooded slope...

The three dogs tugged on ahead of us. We traveled through a windfall for a quarter of a mile, and then came into the stand to find it vacant, and the hounds baying on the slopes, towards the Richland. They had crossed the gap, hounds and hunters, too; for a moment after we heard the musical notes from a horn wound by some one in the lower wilderness. It was wound to tell the standers to pass around the heights to the lofty gaps between the Richland and the waters of the Pigeon.

As was afterwards related, the bear had passed through Eli's stand, but Eli was not there on account of his mistaking and occupying for a drive-way a gully that ended in a precipice on either side of the ridge. He, with the other stander, soon joined us and we pushed along the trail, towards the summit of the Great Divide...

It was past noon, and while we listened to the low baying of the hounds in the depths, we munched at a snack of corn bread and boiled corned beef. In the meantime, Wid was examining the trail from one slope to the other. He would peer closely into every clump of briers, pulling them apart with his hands, and bend so low over the grasses along the path, that the black strip in his light colored trousers, hidden by his brown coat tails when he walked erect, would be exposed to view.

At length he paused and called us to him. The branch of a whortleberry bush, to which he pointed, was freshly broken off, and in the black soft soil, close to the trail, was the visible imprint of a bear's paw. Bruin evidently had a long start on the pack, and having climbed up from the gulf, had passed through Grassy gap, and descended to the Pigeon. We now all fired our guns in order to bring the hunters and hounds as soon as possible to us.

It was 4 o'clock, and the shadows were growing bluer, when up through the laurel tangles, out from under the service-trees, hawthorns, and balsams, came the pack—one dog after another, the first five or six, in quick succession, and the others straggling after. Wid seemed to deliberate a moment about stopping them or not; but, as they raced by, he cut the thongs of the three dogs which we had kept all day, remarking: "Let 'em rip. Hits too late fer us to foller, tho.' We'll hev ter lay by at the Double spring till morning"...

All the hunters soon came straggling in; and as a soft, but cold evening breeze fanned the mountain glorified with the light of fading day, and the vales of the Pigeon grew blue-black under the heavy shadows of the Balsam range, we filed into the cove where bubbles the Double spring, and made preparations for supper and shelter similar to the previous night.

As it grew darker the breeze entirely died away, leaving that dead, awful hush that oftentimes precedes a heavy snow storm…the stripped limbs of ancient beeches, and the white, dead branches of blasted hemlocks, unswayed and noiseless, caught the bright light of the fire. The mournful howl of the wolves from points beyond intervening dismal defiles now and then came through the impenetrable darkness to our ears.

Snow began steadily falling—that soft, flaky sort of snow, which seems to descend without a struggle, continues for hours, and then without warning suddenly ceases. All night it fell, sifting through our ill-constructed shelter, burying us in its white folds and extinguishing the fire…

I awoke to find my legs asleep from the weight of a fellow-sleeper's legs crossed over them. As I sat up, leaning my elbows on the bodies of two mountaineers packed tight against me, I saw the old hunter, on his hands and knees in the snow, bending over a bed of coals surrounded by snow-covered fire-logs. Some live coals, awakened by the hunter's breath, were glowing strong enough for me to thus descry his dark form, and the clear features and puffed cheeks of his face. He had a struggle before the flames sprung up and began drying the wet timbers. It was still dark around us, but a pale, rosy light was beginning to suffuse the sky, from which the storm-clouds had been driven.

While part of the company prepared breakfast, the rest of us picked our way through the shoe-mouth-deep snow to the summit of Cold Spring mountain. It was the prospect of a sunrise on mountains of snow that called us forth. The sky was radiant with light when we reached the desired point; but the sun was still hidden behind the symmetrical summit of Cold mountain…Light was pouring, through an eastern gap, upon the wide vale of the river far to the north. In its bottom lay a silver fog. Snow-mantled mountains embosomed it. It resembled the interior of a great porcelain bowl, with a rim of gold appearing round it as day-light grew stronger. Fifty miles away, with front translucent and steel-blue, stood the Black mountains. Apparently no snow had fallen on them. Their elevated, rambling crest, like the edge of a broken-toothed, cross-cut saw, was visible.

After breakfast we started on the backbone of the Balsam range for the Rich mountain, distant about eight miles. It was a picturesque body of men, that in single file waded in the snow under the burdened balsams, and crawled over the white-topped logs. The head youth from Caney Fork had his hat pulled down so far over his ears, to protect them from the cold, that half of his head, flaunting yellow locks, was exposed above the tattered felt, and only the lower portion of his pale, weak face appeared below the rim. His blue, homespun coat hardly reached the top of his pantaloons; and his great, horny hands, and arms half way to the elbows protruded from torn sleeves… Next behind him came Wid, with his face as red as ever, and his long hair the color of the snow. Then followed Allen, a thick-set, sturdy youth from the Richland. He gloried in his health and vigor, and to show it, wore nothing over his back but a thin muslin shirt. He whistled as he walked, and laughed and halloed till the forests responded, *whenever a balsam branch dislodged its snow upon his head and shoulders. Noah Harrison, another valley farmer, who likes hunting better than farming, came next. He was a matter-of-fact fellow, and showed his disrelish to the snow by picking, with his keen eyes, his steps in the foot-prints of those ahead. Jonas Medford, a stout, mustached son of the old hunter, followed behind…*

When half-way round the ridge, we caught faint echoes from the hounds below. The sound was as stirring in tone as the reveille of the camp. A minute after, our party was broken into sections, every one being left to pick his way as best he could to the scene of the fight between the dogs and bear…A balsam slope is the roughest ever trodden by the foot of man. The rhododendrons and kalmias [laurels] are perfect net-works. In them a man is in as much danger of becoming irrecoverably entangled unto death as a fly in a spider's web; but, in the excitement caused by that faint chiming of the hounds, no one seemed to think of the danger of being lost in the labyrinths.

Luckily, before we three had proceeded 100 yards down a steep declivity, we struck the channel of a tiny brook. Hedges of rhododendron grow rankly along it, on both sides, and almost meet over the clear, rushing water. It would be impossible for a man to penetrate these hedges for any great distance, unless time was of no object whatever. The path of the torrent affords the path for the hunter. We had on rubber boots, and so waded in, following it down a devious course. It was an arduous walk. At times slippery rocks sent us floundering; boulders intercepted us, and the surface of deep pools rose higher than our boot-tops. For two miles we pushed on, our ardor being kept aflame by the increasing noise of the pack, and a few minutes later, we reached the scene of the struggle…of all fights that between a pack of ravenous dogs and a frenzied bear is the most exciting. But few persons are ever accorded a sight of this nature. It can never be forgotten by them. This is what we saw on issuing from the laurel: A white wintry expanse, free from undergrowth, on which the trees were set a little further apart than usual; back of us the stream; while across the open expanse, at the distance of twenty yards, a leaning cliff with the wild vines on its front sprinkled with snow, and its top hidden from view by the giant hemlocks before it. Close at the base of one of these hemlocks, reared on his haunches, sat a shaggy black bear. He was licking his chops; and, holding his fore paws up in approved pugilistic style, was coolly eyeing ten hounds, which, forming a semi-circle, distant about ten feet before him, were baying and barking with uplifted heads and savage teeth exposed. One poor hound, with skull cracked by Bruin's paw, lay within the circle. At the foot of a hemlock near us sat two bleeding curs, and one with a broken leg began dragging himself toward us.

By exposing ourselves we lost our chances for a shot; for, as soon as we came in view, the hounds, encouraged by the sight of men, sprang at their antagonist with redoubled fury and increased yelping. It would have been impossible for us to have made a shot without having killed or disabled several of the hounds; so with triggers cocked we bided our time and with interest watched the combat. Judging by his methods of defense, Bruin was an adept in that line. He had had time for experience, for he was a great, shaggy fellow with gray tufts of hair on his head. He showed his teeth and growled as the dogs kept jumping at him. A twelve hour fight, in which several of the pack had been rendered incapable of attack, had given caution to the remainder, and they were extremely wary about taking their nips at him.

During the melee that for the next minute ensued, one savage hound was caught in the clutches of the bear and hugged and bitten to death; while, taking advantage of the momentary exposure of his sides, the others of the pack fell upon old Bruin until he was completely hidden under the struggling mass. He had just shaken them off again and recovered his balance, when a rifle shot sounded, and a puff of white smoke arose from under a spruce at the edge of the laurel thicket. The noise of the fight had prevented us hearing the approach of Wid, the old hunter. I looked from him at the group. Bruin had fallen forward on his face. Every dog was on his body, now writhing in its death throes…

One by one the hunters straggled in. The animal was skinned where he lay; and then, packed with hide, meat, blankets and our guns, we descended the middle prong of the Pigeon to the road through the picturesque valley.

18

WILLIAM BREWSTER'S EXPLORATION OF THE SOUTHERN APPALACHIAN MOUNTAINS: THE JOURNAL OF 1885

William Brewster

The preeminent nineteenth-century American ornithologist William Brewster (1851–1919) was born in Wakefield, Massachusetts. The youngest son of a Boston banker, he was educated in the public schools of Cambridge, but poor health kept him from attending Harvard University. As his main interest from an early age had been natural history, particularly bird studies, with the support of his father Brewster became an ornithologist at age twenty.

In addition to studying the avifauna of New England with particular care, Brewster also traveled extensively in the United States, conducting important field studies, usually in the company of other naturalists such as Robert Ridgeway, Joel A. Allen and Frank Chapman. During a distinguished career that lasted until the year of his death, he was head of the bird and mammal collections at the Boston Society of Natural History (1879–87); head of bird and mammal collections at Harvard University's Museum of Comparative Zoology (1885–1900); and director of ornithology for the same institution (1900–19).

In 1883, Brewster was a founding member of the American Ornithologists' Union, which grew into the leading organization for scientific ornithology in the United States. He was one of the organizers of the first Audubon Society and served as a director of the National Association of Audubon Societies, which later became the National Audubon Society. In 1919, the American Ornithologists' Union established the William Brewster Medal, awarded to the authors of the most valuable contributions relating to the birds of the Western Hemisphere.

For those interested in the natural history of Western North Carolina, an excursion Brewster made in late May and early June 1885 to the region was especially noteworthy. From a scientific perspective, the trip was significant as it enabled him to establish with certainty that more than twenty bird species—dark-eyed juncos, red-breasted nuthatches, brown creepers, winter wrens, golden-crowned kinglets, black-capped chickadees, etc.— thought at that time to be "Northern" breeders did in fact nest in the higher elevations of the southern mountains. Brewster's scientific observations were presented in *The Auk* in 1886 as "An Ornithological Reconnaissance in Western North Carolina."

Raven.

The meticulous journal he kept was superbly edited by Marcus B. Simpson Jr. and published in the *North Carolina Historical Review* in 1980 as "William Brewster's Exploration of the Southern Appalachian Mountains: The Journal of 1885." It is an appealing document—even for those with only a passing interest in birds—because of Brewster's evocative descriptions of the region.

Simpson summarized the ornithologist's route as follows:

> *Following a period of intense field work around Charleston, South Carolina, Brewster departed by rail for the Carolina mountains on May 22, 1885, passed through Salisbury, and took the Western North Carolina Railroad through Old Fort on his way to Asheville. On May 25, after two days in Asheville, Brewster resumed his trip westward, going by train across the Pigeon River, through Waynesville, across the Great Balsam Mountains at Balsam Gap, and into the Tuckasegee River valley. Leaving the train at Sylva, Brewster traveled by horse and carriage to Webster and thence across the Cowee Mountain to Franklin. On May 27 his carriage party, following the course of the Cullasaja River, ascended the Highlands Plateau, where Brewster found the first solid evidence of northern or boreal birds nesting in the southern Appalachians. On May 29 he departed Highlands and traveled along the Tuckasegee River [through* East Laporte] *to Sylva, where he retraced his route by train, arriving in Asheville on May 30. On June 1 Brewster set out by carriage along the Swannanoa River toward Mount Mitchell and the lofty Black Mountain range. As at Highlands, the Mount*

Mitchell area yielded substantial new evidence of northern species inhabiting the higher elevations of the Carolina mountains. Returning to Asheville on June 2, Brewster packed his notes and specimens and departed for Boston by rail the following day.

The common names for birds mentioned in the text are provided in place of Brewster's scientific nomenclature.

FRANKLIN TO HIGHLANDS

1885 Wednesday May 27. *Cloudy with a steady, pouring rain all day, the mountains wrapped in mist. We left Franklin at 9:30 A.M. and reached Highlands at about 4 P.M. taking lunch by the way in a little unfinished church where we found a secure shelter from the drenching rain. The road for the first six or eight miles followed a winding stream and was comparatively level. Then began the ascent of a steep mountain where, for hours, the horses plodded on at a snail's pace and our party encased in rubber defied the weather as well as possible…The timber on the mountain sides was chiefly deciduous trees, oaks, chestnuts, beeches, and tulip trees predominating, and many of the trees of large size and grand proportions…*

Upon reaching the top of the plateau on which Highlands is located we saw the first Juncos. As we whirled rapidly along the smooth road through open park-like oak woods, [scarlet] *Tanagers,* [rose-breasted] *Grosbeaks, and Solitary Vireos* [now called blue-headed vireos] *were singing on all sides. In the evening Robins were singing everywhere & Hylas peeping in the woods. The scenery during this day's drive was everywhere wild, picturesque, and exceedingly beautiful but nowhere either fine or grand.*

HIGHLANDS

1885 May 28 Thursday…*A.M. clear with cool and rather high wind. Waking at day break I hear a glorious burst of bird music through the open window of my bed room…Immediately after breakfast we started on horseback for Whitesides* [Whiteside Mountain, about three and a half miles northeast of Highlands], *a neighboring mountain of about 5000 ft. elevation. The road after leaving the village plunged down a steep slope and entered a superb rhododendron swamp where many of these shrubs attained a height of 25 ft. They grew in such tangled thickets that it was impossible for anything larger than a cat to get through them and their glossy evergreen foliage presented the appearance of a solid wall of dark green, semi-tropical in aspect. They formed the undergrowth of a forest of superb hemlocks, many of which were three or four feet in diameter and seventy or eighty feet high. The ground beneath was a spongy morass carpeted with green moss (Sphagnum?) and rich in beautiful ferns. In this place the characteristic birds were Veerys (hundreds, making the air ring with their music), Wood Thrush, Black-throated Blue Warbler (hundreds singing incessantly), Chestnut-sided Warbler, Canada Warbler, Louisiana Waterthrush (one singing), Dark-eyed Junco, Brown Creeper (one), two Red-breasted Nuthatch, Blackburnian Warbler (singing everywhere in the tops of the hemlocks), and an occasional* [blue] *Jay screaming overhead or a Pileated Woodpecker uttering its ringing call in the distance…*

The town of Highlands is situated on a nearly level plateau elevation about 4000 ft. Woods chiefly oak and chestnut, the trees of gigantic proportions. Streams invariably bordered by dense rhododendron. Trees often thickly *hung with* Usnea *moss* [actually a lichen, often called "old man's beard"]. *Swamps carpeted with Sphagnum mosses. Leucothoe* [doghobble] *in full bloom bordering the thickets & paths.*

HIGHLANDS TO EAST PORTE, TUCKASEGEE RIVER

1885 May 29…*Leaving Highlands at 9 A.M. we drove to East La Porte* [East Laport is several miles east of Sylva], *which was reached about sunset. The road was an almost continual descent and for about six miles below Hamburg* [the Cashiers area], *steep, rocky, and dangerous, barely six inches from the brink of* [a] *precipice with the Tuckasegee River roaring and rushing in white foam over the rapids hundreds of feet below. Throughout this stretch the scenery was simply superb, the picturesque river, the vertical-clad walls of the canon, and innumerable picturesque falls, rhododendron-clad banks, and grand old woods multiplying the attractions and giving a never ending variety to the landscape. The forests were the finest we have thus far seen. Many of the oaks and tulip trees exceeded five feet in diameter and with their straight column-like trunks and perfectly open ground beneath recalled the forests of the lower Wabash Valley of Illinois.*

The event of the day, ornithologically speaking, was the sight of four Ravens [another Northern species resident in the higher elevations of the southern Appalachians], *the only ones seen on the trip. The first winged its way across the road passing through the oak woods and finally alighting in a tree. This was at about 4000 ft. The other three were together in the woods a mile or two above Hamburg at about 3500 ft. One ascended high into the air, then descended with half-closed wings. The other two left their perches as we passed and flapped across the valley uttering their hoarse* cr-r-ruck *as they flew. All looked* enormous…

ASHEVILLE TO BLACK MOUNTAIN

1885 June 1 Monday…*Cloudless, warm, and a beautiful day. Left Asheville at 8 A.M. in a top buggy drawn by a pair of horses, my destination being the Black Mountain group. For the first twelve miles the road followed the course of the Swannanoa River, a beautiful stream averaging about thirty yards in width, for the most part shallow and rapid, its banks bordered by fine red birches (4 ft. in diameter)* [sweet or black birch, *Betula lenta*], *sycamores, red maples, black walnuts, red oaks, water oaks* [*Quercus nigra* does not grow in Western North Carolina], *etc. with an undergrowth of alders. The larger trees grew out over the water, their tops and branches often meeting and interlacing with those on the opposite banks forming an arch of foliage beneath which the river flowed smoothly and silently in places, in others rushed noisily over ledges or rippled musically down the pebbly shallows…*

We reached our camping ground…after a terribly steep, hard pull for the last two miles…Finally the sun set and as the twilight gathered in the valley below and gradually enveloped the higher slopes and ridges there was a grand chorus of Robins,

Wilson's Thrushes [veeries], *and Snowbirds* [dark-eyed juncos] *for a brief space. Then the stars began to glimmer and twinkle in the steel blue vault above, a wolf howled dismally on the ridge above and night closed over the scene as we wrapped ourselves in or blankets and made preparations for the night.*

BLACK MOUNTAINS

1885 Tuesday June 2…Clear and a perfect day. Awakening at 4 A.M. I found the eastern horizon was beginning to flush while overhead the moon gleamed like a piece of silver in the clear but still dusky heaven…At 4:30 the first Wilson's Thrush joined the chorus then another lower down the mountain began its song. The keen, almost frosty wind swept past over the mountain side chilling me as I listened, drowning some of the bird voices, bringing others from ridges far away.

5 A.M…The light over the eastern ridge had gradually become stronger bringing out details of trees, rocks, and the outline of neighboring ridges, but the great gulf or "cove" below was still wrapped in gloom, the distant low country and mountains in pale bluish haze…I saddled my mare and was soon on my way to the summit. For about a mile and a half the path wound its way upward usually in zig-zags after the usual fashion of trails in this region. It was walled by young firs and spruces while the larger trees of the same species cast a dense, gloomy shade rarely penetrated by a shaft of sunlight…

Upon reaching the summit I found myself on a long narrow ridge stretching miles away on a nearly perfect level and rarely more than twenty yards in width. On this ridge rise several peaks elevated from four to six hundred feet above the general elevation of the ridge, which is close on 6000 ft. (my barometer made it 5950 ft.). For the last half mile I noticed a gradual deterioration in the size of the firs and spruces and on the summit of the ridge they were very appreciably stunted, none being over forty feet high and twelve feet in diameter. Black spruces [red spruce, *Picea rubens*] *predominated with however a larger admixture of balsams than was seen elsewhere. There were also many yellow birches and an occasional rhododendron. Many of the trees were dead and bleached, in places standing in grim groups, in others prostrate and heaped on one another in tangled masses, with vigorous young saplings growing up to conceal the ruin beneath. The ground was rough and rocky but rocks, boulders, logs, and crevices were alike carpeted with yellowish-green sphagnum soaked with water by the recent rains…*

At about 10 A.M. we started down the mountain…we reached Wm Glass's at noon and after dining started for Asheville where we arrived at about six o'clock. The return drive down the valley of the river Swannanoa was charming for the river was at its loveliest in the clear afternoon light and long shadows from the mountains stretched over the fields of grain and the emerald meadows bordering the stream. The birds were singing freely and there was a delicious ripe, mellow quality in the air such as we occasionally notice in New England in October. Altogether it was a fair picture—such a picture in fact as no one fond of nature could look on without a keen sense of enjoyment. It was a fitting close to a delightful and successful trip for with this day ended my season in North Carolina.

19

THE LETTERS OF JOHN S. CAIRNS TO WILLIAM BREWSTER, 1887–1895

John S. Cairns

The systematic observation of birds in Western North Carolina did not commence until May 22, 1885. That's the day Harvard Professor William Brewster stepped off a coach of the Western North Carolina Railroad in Asheville. The story of his "ornithological reconnaissance" of the Balsams, the Highlands Plateau and Mount Mitchell is delineated in a previous selection.

During that venture, Brewster verified the existence of numerous breeding birds in the high southern mountains (rose-breasted grosbeaks, Blackburnian and Canada warblers, veeries, etc.) that had previously been presumed to breed only many hundreds of miles to the north. He also observed that two of the birds breeding here—the blue-headed vireo (then called the solitary vireo) and the dark-eyed junco—differed enough from the Northern species to be described taxonomically as southern Appalachian subspecies.

While exploring Western North Carolina, Brewster did not know there was a resident ornithologist living at Weaverville, several miles north of Asheville—one who had been conducting year-round observations on his own initiative. His name was John S. Cairns, he was twenty-three years old and he, too, had a passion for birds.

After reading an article titled "The Summer Birds of Buncombe County, North Carolina" that Cairns contributed in 1889 to *Ornithologist and Oologist*, Brewster wrote the young birder, initiating a scientific and personal correspondence that lasted until Cairns's untimely death in 1895. The eminent Harvard professor and the business manager of a family-owned mill in the Carolina mountains had found common ground.

John S. Cairns (1862–1895) was born in Lawrence, Massachusetts. His parents had migrated in 1855 from Scotland to the United States, where the elder Cairns served as foreman of various textile mills in New England. The family moved to Weaverville in 1870 and purchased Reems Creek Woolen Mills. Cairns married Lena Cressman in 1888. He served as secretary and business manager of the mill until his death.

On the morning of June 10, 1895, Cairns and a group of friends and family pitched camp high in the Black Mountains. He left the camp and hiked toward Mount Mitchell to collect specimens for Brewster. When he failed to return by the agreed-upon time, a

Black-Throated Blue Warbler.

search party was sent out. His body was found the following morning. According to one account, Cairns's gun discharged while he was using it to dislodge a fungus from a tree; another account has the gun discharging when it fell after having been propped against a tree.

No one seems to know just how or why Cairns developed his love for and knowledge of birds. But at a very early age—when he was not yet ten years old—he began exploring the Great Craggy and Black Mountains while they were truly wilderness areas. Marcus B. Simpson Jr. summarized his accomplishments in a profile written for the *Dictionary of North Carolina Biography* in 1979:

> *His observations provided the best available description of the avifauna of the North Carolina mountains before extensive disruption of the original forests by human activities. He added over a dozen bird species to the state list and corresponded with many of the world's eminent zoologists, providing them with documentary specimens and important data to zoological collections...In 1889, Cairns was elected an associate member of the American Ornithologists' Union, and in 1894–1895 he served on the advisory council of the World's Congress on Ornithology.*

In 1897, Cairns became the first North Carolina resident to have a bird species named in his honor. The Cairns warbler (*Dendroica caerulescens cairnsi*) is a subspecies of the beautiful black-throated blue warbler that nests only in the high mountains of Western North Carolina and adjacent regions.

Cairns privately published an eighteen-page pamphlet titled *List of the Birds of Buncombe County, North Carolina* in 1891. It is the best available record as to how significantly the bird life of Western North Carolina has changed in just over a century: Bewick's wrens were then "common" (now rarely seen); a flock of forty pelicans appeared on the French Broad in May 1889; American bitterns were then "tolerably common" (now only very occasional); black rails nested in the wet meadows along the rivers (scarcely ever seen again); swallow-tailed kites were seen each season (now very rarely seen); golden eagles were breeding "on the cliffs" (their status today is uncertain, but they're certainly not a breeding species); barn swallows were then "rare" (now very common); warbling vireos were "tolerably common" (now only occasional); and so on.

Specimens of birds, eggs and nests that Cairns shipped to Brewster after receiving his initial letter complemented the professional ornithologist's personal observations and helped lay the foundation for our present understanding of the birds of the southern Appalachians in general and Western North Carolina in particular. Cairns's correspondence with Brewster—despite his unconventional syntax, capitalization and spelling—is informative and delightful. It was edited by Simpson and published in 1978 as "The Letters of John S. Cairns to William Brewster, 1887–1895" in the *North Carolina Historical Review*. Reproduced here are portions of four of the twenty-seven letters contained in that publication. All of them were addressed from "Weaverville, N.C."

> *Jan. 31—87.*
> *Mr. William Brewster,*
> *Dear Sir,*
> *Your letter dully rec'd.*
> *In regard to the list of birds in last O&O [Ornithologist and Oologist] judging from your letter their must be some mistakes. I cannot tell how many, as I have not rec'd the last issue of O&O...The Snowy Owl I have never taken my self. I saw one that was*

shot 9 miles east of Asheville. Whether the skin was preserved or not I can not tell, as I was unable to get the bird. I have also seen two specimens on the mts five miles east from here, one in 1884 and one in 85 and have been lately informed that the same bird had returned. [As noted by Simpson, "The Snowy Owl…resides in northern Canada and rarely winters southward to North Carolina. Cairns was the first to discover its occurrence in the mountains."]…

I am Very Truly Yours
Jno. S. Cairns

Feb 11th 87
Mr. William Brewster,
Dear Sir,
Your kind letter of Feb 4th rec'd. Was glad to hear that my skins proved all right. I have not got any more specimens like the Thrush I sent you, but I will try to get you some in the spring. The eggs were spoted when I found them, though they are plain now, as I got them wet soon after I found them and the spots all came off. The spots were of dark redish brown color, and from the size of a No 5 shot. I am positive the bird was not Willsons Thrush [that is, the high-elevation breeding thrush now known as the veery]…*Any thing I can do for you here will give me great pleasure. I will be glad to exchange specimens for books on ornithology, eggs or skins. Please make out a list of what you want. I will go to Craggy and Black Mountains several times the coming summer and spring. I always get something new their. I would like to have seen you, when you was in Asheville last summer, but I did not know anything about it until you was gone…Your kind letter is worth much more to me then the few skins I sent you. Hopeing to hear from you soon I am*

Very truly Yours
Jno. S Cairns

June 16 1887
Mr Brewster,
Dear Sir,
In regard to nest of Mtn S.V. [mountain solitary vireo, now called blue-headed vireo] *you may describe it if you wish. The nest was found on the south side of the Mtn about 200 feet from the top, in a beautiful grove of Beech and Chestnut timber.* [As noted by Simpson, "This was the first nest discovered of the Mountain Solitary Vireo (*Vireo solitarius alticola*), the local subspecies described earlier by Brewster."] *I seen an other pair, but could not find their nest. Will try and go to the Black Mtn this month. I heard and seen a number of thrushes when on Craggy, but none like the one I got last year. The weather was very cold and windy their and the birds did not seem to be on the move, and very shy…Mean while I will do my best for you here and get to the mts soon as I can…*

Yours truly, Jno. S. Cairns

August 1 87
Mr William B
Kind friend,
Your letter recd. I do not wish to part with the set [eggs] *of Rails, but will be happy to give*
you two of them for the trouble you have taken with me…I have read your paper on the birds
of western No. Car several times, and find it very interesting…Where did you find the Wood
Duck? I have hunted in vain for it and have never taken a single specimen since I began to
study Ornithology…Did you see the nests of the Purple Grackles when in Asheville? I have
frequently seen them their the last of May, but never afterwards. Where did you find the
Duck Hawk [peregrine falcon]*? It is very rare here in this county. Have only observed*
two specimens here. Who were your informers in regard to the Wild Piegon pasing through
in numbers, and in what countys did they ocour in? They used to pass through in numbers,
but of late years they have intirely stoped coming. Have only observed one bird the past four
years. [As noted by Simpson, "The Wild Pigeon or Passenger Pigeon (*Ectopistes migratorius*) was one of the most abundant species in America until the late 1800s, when human activities drove the bird into extinction. The species occurred in North Carolina during the winter months in flocks numbering in the millions. Cairns's observations in the mountains spanned the period of the bird's precipitous decline and disappearance."] *The Sparrow* [American kestrel] *and Sharp Shin*[n]*ed Hawks breed here as have taken their eggs. The Bald Eagle*
also breeds, I think. Saw two young in Asheville last year, and was informed that they were
taken about 30 miles South of A____. I find that certain species of birds range much higher
of Cragy Mtn than on Black. Have found Rose Breasted Grosbeaks, Golden crowned
Thrushes [golden-crowned kinglets] *nearly 6,000 feet and once took a cat Bird on the*
highest point of Craggy, while on the Black have never observed them higher than the line of
Firs. I find the skins of the Black thro Blue W. that I got at Black Mtn are much smaller and
pailer blue than specimens taken during the spring migration. [As Simpson noted, "This statement was the first recognition that the local population of Black-throated Blue Warbler were morphologically distinct from the northern forms."]…*Did*
you here any thing about the Swallow-Tailed Kite, in the western countys? Have been told that
it did ocour in numbers in Yancy & Mitchell [Counties]. *Have observed it twice on Elk*
Mtn, both times in August. [As Simpson noted, "The Swallow-tailed Kite (*Elanoides forficatus*) formerly nested in the coastal plain swamps and along the Mississippi River Valley. By Cairns's day the species was declining rapidly in numbers. These and several earlier reports are the only evidence that the species occurred as a fall transient in the North Carolina mountains"]…*I may possibly*
get to the Black Mts this week, as some friends are going and want me to go with them. I
don't expect to collect much this time, though I'll keep my eyes open for any thing new. I inclose
Photo. Excuse the appearance of my hair as it wont stay com[b]*ed & the Photographer*
would not al[l]*ow me to wet it nor use a brush. So you see the result. Am 25 years old, am of*
Scotch desent, and was born in Mass. So you see I'm a Yankey and not a tar healer—Hoping
to hear from you soon & that the Rail eggs will prove to be Black R[ail]*. I am very Sincerely*
JSC

20

ON HORSEBACK (1888)

Charles Dudley Warner

Essayist, novelist, travel writer and editor Charles Dudley Warner (1829–1900) was born in Plainfield, Massachusetts. He became an influential editor of *Harper's Magazine*. But he is perhaps best remembered in American literary history for his close friendship with Mark Twain. Warner was the first to coin the observation, "Everybody complains about the weather, but nobody *does* anything about it," which was quoted by Twain in a lecture and often attributed to the more famous writer.

Warner's finest book is perhaps *My Summer in a Garden* (1870), but he also penned a number of travel books, several of which are of enduring interest. This description of his travels in Western North Carolina initially appeared in the September 1885 issue of the *Atlantic Monthly* and was included in *On Horseback*, which was published in 1888.

The outing commenced at Abingdon in the far southwestern tip of Virginia. From there, Warner and a friend he addressed as "The Professor" traveled down the valley of the Holston River into Tennessee, and then over the mountains into North Carolina. Throughout the journey they lodged mostly in private homes, where Warner recorded with some skill (albeit with considerable regional arrogance) the lifestyles observed.

From Boone they proceeded "through noble growths of oaks, chestnuts, hemlocks, and rhododendrons" to Valle Crucis, which, according to Warner, consisted of a "blacksmith shop and a dirty, fly-blown store." After making stops at Banner Elk, Hanging Rock, Cranberry Forge, Roan Mountain and Bakersville, they arrived at Burnsville on their way to Asheville. Nearby, on the western flank of Mount Mitchell, they located the farmstead of Big Tom Wilson, one of the most colorful and famous hunting guides and local characters of the late nineteenth century.

Big Tom was born in a cabin on the Toe River in Yancey County in 1825. In 1852 he married a young woman with the wonderful name of Niagra Ray. The next year they moved to a cabin on the headwaters of the Cane River, where he served as gamekeeper for a vast tract of virgin wilderness known as the Murchison Preserve.

Observing that "not to see him was to miss one of the most characteristic productions of the country, the typical backwoods-man, hunter, and guide," Warner described "Big

On Horseback in the Mountains.

Tom's plantation" as "an open-work stable, an ill-put-together frame house, with two rooms and a kitchen, and a veranda in front, a loft, and a spring-house in the rear. Chickens and other animals have free run of the premises. Some fish-rods hung in the porch, and hunter's gear depended on hooks in the passage-way to the kitchen. In one room were three beds, in the other two, only one in the kitchen. On the porch was a loom, with a piece of cloth in process. The establishment had the air of taking care of itself."

As is often the instance with memorable personalities, Big Tom's most striking attribute was his spiritual vitality, not his physicality. Warner noted,

> [He] *would not attract attention from his size. He is six feet and two inches tall, very spare and muscular, with sandy hair, a long gray beard and honest blue eyes. He has a reputation for great strength and endurance; a man of native simplicity and mild manners…There was an entire absence of braggadocio in Big Tom's talk, but somehow, as he went on, his backwoods figure loomed larger and larger in our imagination, and he seemed strangely familiar. At length it came over us where we had met him before. It was in Cooper's novels. He was the Leather-Stocking exactly. And yet he was an original; for he assured us that he had never read the "Leather-Stocking Tales."*

Wilson convinced his guests that it was worthwhile to climb nearby Mount Mitchell, the highest peak in Eastern North America, at 6,684 feet, to obtain the view and visit the grave of Dr. Elisha Mitchell, who died on the mountaintop after a fall. (See the Elisha Mitchell selection in this anthology.) This is perhaps the most interesting episode in *On Horseback*. Warner provided a detailed description of their ascent via "steep hillsides and through gullies, over treacherous sink-holes in the rocks, through quaggy places, heaps of brush, and rotten logs." He concluded with a moving description of Elisha Mitchell's last resting place and a memorable, if bombastic, description of a mighty thunderstorm they encountered atop the mountain.

> *From Wilson's to the peak of Mitchell it is seven and a half miles; we made it in five and a half hours…What a magnificent forest! Oaks, chestnut, poplars, hemlocks, the cucumber (a species of magnolia, with a pinkish, cucumber-like cone), and all sorts of northern and southern growths meeting here in splendid array…*
>
> *As we approached the top, Big Tom pointed out the direction, a half mile away, of a small pond, a little mountain tarn, overlooked by a ledge of rock, where Professor Mitchell lost his life. Big Tom was the guide that found his body…*
>
> *The summit is a nearly level spot of some thirty or forty feet in extent either way, with a floor of rock and loose stones. The stunted balsams have been cut away so as to give a view. The sweep of prospect is vast, and we could see the whole horizon except in the direction of Roan, whose long bulk was enveloped in cloud. Portions of six States were in sight, we were told, but that is merely a geographical expression. What we saw, wherever we looked, was an inextricable tumble of mountains, without order*

or leading line of direction—domes, peaks, ridges, endless and countless, everywhere, some in shadow, some tipped with shafts of sunlight, all wooded and green or black, and all in more softened contours than our Northern hills, but still wild, lonesome, terrible. Away in the southwest, lifting themselves up in a gleam of the western sky, the Great Smoky Mountains loomed like a frowning continental fortress, sullen and remote. With Clingman and Gibbs and Holdback peaks near at hand and apparently of equal height, Mitchell seemed only a part and not separate from the mighty congregation of giants.

In the centre of the stony plot on the summit lie the remains of Mitchell. To dig a grave in the rock was impracticable, but the loose stones were scooped away to the depth of a foot or so, the body was deposited, and the stones were replaced over it. It was the original intention to erect a monument, but the enterprise of the projectors of this royal entombment failed at that point. The grave is surrounded by a low wall of loose stones, to which each visitor adds one, and in the course of ages the cairn may grow to a good size. The explorer lies there without name or headstone to mark his awful resting-place. The mountain is his monument. He is alone with its majesty. He is there in the clouds, in the tempests, where the lightnings play, and thunders leap, amid the elemental tumult, in the occasional great calm and silence and the pale sunlight. It is the most majestic, the most lonesome grave on earth.

As we sat there, awed a little by this presence, the clouds were gathering from various quarters and drifting towards us. We could watch the process of thunderstorms and of tempests. I have often noticed on other high mountains how the clouds, forming like genii released from the earth, mount into the upper air, and in masses of torn fragments of mist hurry across the sky as to a rendezvous of witches. This was a different display. These clouds came slowly sailing from the distant horizon, like ships on an aerial voyage. Some were below us, some on our level; they were all in well-defined, distinct masses, molten silver on deck, below trailing rain, and attended on earth by gigantic shadows that moved with them. This strange fleet of battle-ships, drifted by the shifting currents, was manœuvering for an engagement. One after another, as they came into range about our peak of observation, they opened fire. As sharp flashes of lightning darted from one to the other, a jet of flames from one leaped across the interval and was buried in the bosom of its adversary; and at every discharge the boom of great guns echoed through the mountains. It was something more than a royal salute to the tomb of the mortal at our feet, for the masses of cloud were rent in the fray, at every discharge the rain was precipitated in increasing torrents, and soon the vast bulks were trailing torn fragments and wreaths of mists, like the shot-away shrouds and sails of ships in battle. Gradually, from this long range practice with single guns and exchange of broadsides, they drifted into closer conflict, rushed together, and we lost sight of the individual combatants in the general tumult of the aerial war.

21

A WORLD OF GREEN HILLS (1898)

Bradford Torrey

Naturalist and writer Bradford Torrey (1843–1912) was born in Weymouth, Massachusetts. Remembered primarily as a nature essayist and close observer of bird life, he did have, as Felton Gibbons and Deborah Storm observed in *Neighbors to the Birds: A History of Birdwatching in America* (1988), "a many-sided career, first in missionary work, then as an editor of *Youth's Companion* and of Thoreau's journals."

From the late 1880s until his death in Santa Barbara, California, where he resided in a boardinghouse (not in "an isolated cabin," as reported in various sources), Torrey traveled widely in the United States to North Carolina, Virginia, New Hampshire, Tennessee, Florida, Arizona and California. These journeys and his observations were initially recreated in articles written for the *Atlantic Monthly* and other publications. After revision, the materials appeared in the thirteen books of nature writing published during his lifetime.

In an insightful overview of Torrey's life and work, Kevin E. O'Donnell noted that as "a close observer of nature, and a master of the 'ramble' when that literary form was at the height of its popularity, Torrey blended the nature ramble with travel writing and ornithology, to introduce readers to emerging vacation destinations in the United States… just as vacation travel was becoming more affordable for middle class Americans."

O'Donnell also pointed out, "During the years covered by Torrey's career, bird-watching went from being an unusual hobby, practiced by a few Americans, to become a widespread practice, endorsed as part of school curricula across the country."

The great nineteenth-century naturalist John Burroughs described Torrey—a lifelong bachelor—as "a fine-souled fellow [who] suggests a bird with his bright eyes and shy ways and sensitiveness."

Published in 1898, *A World of Green Hills* is divided into two parts, equally devoted to travels in Western North Carolina and southwestern Virginia (Pulaski and Natural Bridge). The North Carolina portion of Torrey's journey was primarily in the area of the Highlands Plateau, which he accessed from Walhalla in upcountry South Carolina via a horse- and mule-drawn wagon.

Blue-Headed Vireo.

He had been, in part, inspired by the prior ornithological journey to the region by his friend, the Harvard University Professor William Brewster, who in May 1885 had discovered many birds whose previously known breeding ranges were far to the north: rose-breasted grosbeaks, blackburnian and black-throated blue warblers, olive-sided flycatchers and others. (See the William Brewster and John S. Cairns selections in this anthology.) Following up on that lead, Torrey took another look at the habitat, no doubt hoping to find additional "Northern" breeders or even a new subspecies.

Torrey, who was also a competent botanist and plant enthusiast, was obviously both surprised and delighted with the level of botanical knowledge displayed by various residents he encountered along the way. Because, in my own experience, this keen interest in plants still prevails on the Highlands Plateau more than a century later, I have included several of his botanical encounters in the following selection.

A turn or two in the road, and we had left the village [Walhalla] *behind us, and then, almost before I knew it, we were among the hills: now aloft on the shoulder of one of them, with innumerable mountains crowding the horizon; now shut in some narrow, winding valley, our "distance and horizon gone," with a bird singing from the bushes, and likely enough a stream playing hide-and-seek behind a tangle of rhododendron and laurel…*

It was after eight o'clock when we turned a sharp corner in the road and saw the lights of the village [Highlands] *shining through the forest ahead of us. In fifteen minutes more I was at supper. I had come a long way by faith…and my faith had not been vain…*

Anthropology and ornithology were very agreeably mingled for me on the Hamburg [Cashiers] *road…The human interview to which I look back with most pleasure was with a pair of elderly people who appeared one morning in an open buggy. They were driving from the town, seated side by side in the shadow of a big umbrella, and as they overtook me, on the bridge, the man said "Good-morning," of course, and then, to my surprise, pulled up his horse and inquired particularly after my health…Then, after a word or two about the beauty of the morning, and while I was still trying to guess who the couple could be, the man gathered up the reins with the remark, "I'm going after some* Ilex monticola *for Charley." "Yes, I know where it is," he added, in response to a question. Then I knew him. I had been at his house a few evenings before to see his son, who had come home from Biltmore to collect certain rare local plants—the mountain holly being one of them—for the Vanderbilt herbarium* [part of the Biltmore House estate in Asheville]. *The mystery was cleared, but it may be imagined how taken aback I was when this venerable rustic stranger threw a Latin name at me.*

In truth, however, botany and Latin names might almost be said to be in the air at Highlands. A villager met me in the street, one day, and almost before I knew it, we were discussing the specific identity of the small yellow lady's-slippers—whether there were two species, or, as my new acquaintance believed, only one, in the woods round about. [Most botanists currently recognize two forms (small and large) of yellow lady's-slipper: *Cypripedium calceolus* variant *parviflorum* and *C.c.* variant *pubescens*.]

Red-Breasted Nuthatch.

At another time, having called at a very pretty unpainted cottage—all the prettier for the natural color of the weathered shingles—I remarked to the lady of the house upon the beauty of Azalea vaseyi, *which I had noticed in several dooryards, and which was said to have been transplanted from the woods. I did not understand why it was, I told her, but I couldn't find it described in my Chapman's* Flora. [A.W. Chapman's *Flora of the Southern United States* had been published in 1860. *Azalea vaseyi*, pink shell azalea, now classified as *Rhododendron vaseyi*, is a Blue Ridge endemic found in a few counties in Western North Carolina and no place else in the world.]

"Oh, it is there, I am sure it is," she answered; and going into the next room she brought out a copy of the manual, turned to the page, and showed me the name. It was in the supplement where in my haste I had overlooked it. I wondered how often, in a New England country village, a stranger could happen into a house, painted or unpainted, and by any chance find the mistress of it prepared to set him right on a question of local botany.

On a later occasion—for thus encouraged I called more than once afterward at the same house—the lady handed me an orchid. I might be interested in it; it was not very common, she believed. I looked at it, thinking at first that I had never seen it before. Then I seemed to remember something.

"Is it Pogonia verticillata.*" I asked.* [The large whorled pogonia, an orchid now classified as *Isotria verticillata*.]

She smiled, and said it was; and when I told her that to the best of my recollection I had never seen more than one specimen before, and that upwards of twenty years ago (a specimen from Blue Hill, Massachusetts), she insisted upon believing that I must have an extraordinary botanical memory, though of course she did not put the compliment thus baldly, but dressed it in some graceful, unanswerable, feminine phrase which I, for all my imaginary mnemonic powers, have long ago forgotten.

The same lady had the rare Shortia galacifolia *growing—transplanted—in her grounds, and her husband volunteered to show me one of the few places in the neighborhood of Highlands (this, too, on his own land) where the true lily-of-the-valley—identical with the European plant of our gardens—grows wild. It was something I had greatly desired to see, and was now in bloom.* [For *Shortia*'s history, see the Michaux selection in this anthology.]

*Still another man—but he was only a summer cottager—took me to look at a specimen of the Carolina hemlock (*Tsuga caroliniana*), a tree of the very existence of which I had before been ignorant.* [Yet another Blue Ridge endemic that displays larger cones than the common eastern hemlock, *Tsuga canadensis*.] *The truth is that the region is most exceptionally rich in its flora, and the people, to their honor be it recorded, are equally exceptional in that they appreciate the fact…*

My arrival at Highlands seemed to have been coincident with that of an extraordinary throng of rose-breasted grosbeaks. For the first few days, especially, the whole countryside was alive with them, till I felt as if I had never seen grosbeaks before. Their warbling was incessant; so incessant, and at the same time so exceedingly smooth and sweet—"mellifluous" is precisely the word—that I welcomed it almost as a relief when the greater part of the chorus moved on. After such a surfeit of honeyed fluency, I was prepared better than ever to appreciate certain of our humbler musicians—with a touch of roughness in the voice and something of brokenness in the tune; birds, for instance, like the black-throated green warbler, the yellow-throated vireo, and the scarlet tanager. But if I was glad the crowd had gone, I was glad also that a goodly sprinkling of the birds had remained; so that there was never a day when I did not see and hear them. The rose-breast is a lovely singer. In my criticism of him I am to be understood as meaning no more than this: that he, like every other artist, has the defects of his good qualities. Smoothness is a virtue in music as in writing; but it is not the only virtue, nor the one that wears longest…

At Highlands the birds were a mixed lot, Southerners and Northerners delightfully jumbled: a few Carolina wrens (one was heard whistling from the summit of Whiteside!); a single Bewick's wren, singing and dodging along a fence in the heart of the village; tufted titmice; Carolina chickadees; Louisiana water thrushes and turkey buzzards: and on the other side of the account, brown creepers, red-bellied [red-breasted] nuthatches, black-throated blues, Canada warblers, Blackburnians, snow-birds [juncos], and olive-sided flycatchers…

As universal time is reckoned—if it is reckoned—old Satulah [the mountain on which Highlands is located] and all that forest-covered world which I saw, or thought I saw, from it, were but of yesterday, a divine improvisation, and would be gone to-morrow…Better even than this wild Satulah garden was a smaller one nearer home: a triangular hillside, broad at the base and pointed at the top, as if it were one face of a pyramid; covered loosely with grand old trees—oaks, chestnuts, and maples; the ground densely matted with freshly grown ferns, largely the cinnamon osmunda [cinnamon fern, Osmunda cinnamomea], clusters of lively green and warm brown intermixed; and everywhere, under the trees and above the ferns, mountain laurel and flame-colored azalea—the laurel blooms pale pink, almost white, and the azalea clusters yellow of every conceivable degree of depth and brightness. A zigzag fence bounded the wood below, and the land rose at a steep angle, so that the whole was held aloft, as it were, for the beholder's convenience. It was a wonder of beauty, with nothing in the least to mar its perfection—the fairest piece of earth my eye ever rested upon. The human owner of it, Mr. Selleck (why should I not please myself by naming him, a land-owner who knew the worth of his possession!), had asked me to go and see it; and for his sake and its own, as well as for my own sake and the reader's, I wish I could show it as it was. It rises before me at this moment…and will do so, I hope, to my dying day.

SOURCES

Primary Sources

Adair, James. *The History of the American Indians; Particularly Those Nations Adjoining to the Mississippi, East and West Florida, Georgia, South and North Carolina. Containing an Account of Their Origin, Language, Manners, Religious and Civil Customs, Laws, Form of Government, Punishments, Conduct in War and Domestic Life, Their Habits, Diet, Agriculture, Manufactures, Diseases and Method of Cure, and Other Particulars, Sufficient to Render it A Complete Indian Systems with Observations on Former Historians, the Conduct of Our Colony, Governors, Superintendents, Missionaries, &C.* London: Printed for Edward and Charles Dilly, in the Poultry, 1775. Reissued. Samuel Cole Williams, ed., Johnson City, TN: Watauga Press, 1930. Kathryn E. Holland Braund, ed., Tuscaloosa: University of Alabama Press, 2005. Online at Library of Congress's "American Memory"—http://memory.loc.gov/cgi-bin/query/r?ammem/faw:@field(DOCID+icufawcbc0005).

Avery, Myron H., and Kenneth S. Boardman, eds. "Arnold Guyot's Notes on the Geography of the Mountain District of Western North Carolina." *North Carolina Historical Review* 15 (July 1938).

Bartram, William. *Travels Through North & South Carolina, Georgia, East & West Florida, the Cherokee Country, the Extensive Territories of the Muscogulges, or Creek Confederacy, and the Country of the Chactaws; Containing An Account of the Soil and Natural Productions of Those Regions, Together with Observations on the Manners of the Indians.* Philadelphia: James & Johnson, 1791. Reissued as *The Travels of William Bartram* ("Naturalist's Edition" with annotations), Francis Harper, ed., New Haven, CT: Yale University Press, 1958. Online at "Documenting the American South"—http://docsouth.unc.edu/nc/bartram/bartram.html.

Battle, Kemp P., ed. *Diary of a Geological Tour by Dr. Elisha Mitchell in 1827 and 1828.* "James Sprunt Historical Monograph No. 6." Chapel Hill: University of North Carolina, 1905. Online at "New River Notes: Historical and Genealogical Resources for the Upper New River Valley of North Carolina and Virginia"—http://www.newrivernotes.com/nc/mitchdia.htm.

Colton, Henry E. *Mountain Scenery: The Scenery of Western North Carolina and Northwestern South Carolina.* Raleigh, NC: W.L. Pomeroy, and Philadelphia: Hayes & Zell, 1859. Online at "Documenting the American South"—http://docsouth.unc.edu/nc/colton/colton.html.

Ewan, Joseph, and Nesta Ewan, eds. "John Lyon, Nurseryman and Plant Hunter, and His Journal, 1799–1814." *Transactions of the American Philosophical Society* 53 (1963).

King, Edward. *The Great South: A Record of Journeys in Louisiana, Texas, the Indian Territory, Missouri, Arkansas, Mississippi, Alabama, Georgia, Florida, South Carolina, North Carolina, Kentucky, Tennessee, Virginia, West Virginia, and Maryland.* Hartford, CT: American Publishing Co., 1875. Published simultaneously in London, England, as *The Southern States of North America.* Reissued by Magruder Drake and Robert R. Jones, eds., Baton Rouge: Louisiana State University Press, 1972. Online at "Documenting the American South"—http://docsouth.unc.edu/nc/king/king.html.

Lanman, Charles. *Letters from the Alleghany Mountains.* New York: G.P. Putnam, 1849. Collected in vol. 1 of *Adventures in the Wilds of the United States and British Provinces,* Charles Lanman. Philadelphia: John W. Moore, 1856. Online at "Making of America Books"—http://quod.lib.umich.edu/m/moa.

Lewis, Jehu. "The Grandfather of North Carolina." *Lakeside Monthly* 10 (September 1873). In *Seekers of Scenery: Travel Writing from Southern Appalachia (1840–1900),* edited by Kevin E. O'Donnell and Helen Hollingsworth. Knoxville: University of Tennessee Press, 2004.

Muir, John. *A Thousand-Mile Walk to the Gulf.* Edited by William Frederic Bade. Boston: Houghton Mifflin Co., 1916. First publication of Muir's 1867 nature notebook. Online at the Sierra Club's "John Muir Exhibit"—http://www.sierraclub.org/john_muir_exhibit/frameindex.html?http://www.sierraclub.org/john_muir_exhibit/writings/a_thousand_mile_walk_to_the_gulf.

"R., of Tennessee," pseudonym of unknown author. "A Week in the Great Smoky Mountains." *The Southern Literary Messenger* 31 (August 1860). In *Appalachian Images in Folk and Popular Culture,* edited by W.K. McNeil. Ann Arbor: University of Michigan Research Press, 1989; reissued Knoxville: University of Tennessee Press, 1995. Online at "Making of America Journals"—http://quod.lib.umich.edu/m/moa.

"Reid, Christian," pseudonym of Frances Christine Fisher Tiernan. "The Mountain-Region of North Carolina." *Appletons' Journal* 2 (1877). Online at "Making of America Journal Articles"—http://quod.lib.umich.edu/m/moa.

Sargent, C.S. "Portions of the Journal of André Michaux, Botanist, Written During His Travels in the United States and Canada, 1785 to 1796." *Proceedings of the American Philosophical Society* 26 (1889). Michaux's manuscript journal, in nine volumes, is deposited in the archives of the American Philosophical Society, Philadelphia.

Simpson, Marcus B., Jr., ed. "The Letters of John S. Cairns to William Brewster, 1887–1895." *North Carolina Historical Review* 55 (Summer 1978). Cairns's letters deposited in Brewster Papers, Archives, Museum of Comparative Zoology, Harvard University.

————, ed. "William Brewster's Exploration of the Southern Appalachian Mountains: The Journal of 1885." *North Carolina Historical Review* 57 (January 1980). Brewster's journal, "The Mountains of North Carolina," deposited in Archives Library, Museum of Comparative Zoology, Harvard University.

Spangenberg, Augustus Gottlieb. "The Spangenberg Diary." *Records of the Moravians in North Carolina* 1, edited by Adelaide L. Fries. Raleigh: North Carolina Historical Association, 1922. Online at "The Colonial Records Project"—http://www.ah.dcr. state.nc.us/sections/hp/colonial/Bookshelf/Moravian/diary.htm.

Strother, John. "Strother's Survey Diary," 1799. Originally filed in the *Suit of the Virginia, Tennessee & Carolina Steel and Iron Company vs. Newman* in the United States Court at Asheville, North Carolina. Subsequently transferred from Asheville in the 1930s (as part of the W. Vance Brown Collection) to the North Carolina Historical Commission, Raleigh, NC. Summarized in *Western North Carolina: A History (from 1730 to 1913)*, John Preston Arthur, Asheville, NC: Edward Buncombe Chapter of the Daughters of the American Revolution, 1914. Reprinted in *The State* (Raleigh, NC), May 1 and May 15, 1966. Online in Explorations section of "Appalachian Summit"—http://appalachiansummit.tripod.com.

Torrey, Bradford. *A World of Green Hills: Observations of Nature and Human Nature in the Blue Ridge.* Boston: Houghton Mifflin and Company, 1888. Online at "Kellscraft Studio"—http://www.kellscraft.com/AWorldofGreenHills/AWorldofGreenHillsContentPage.html.

Warner, Charles Dudley. *On Horseback: A Tour in Virginia, North Carolina, and Tennessee with Notes of Travel in Mexico and California.* Boston and New York: Houghton, Mifflin, and Company, 1888.

Wood, Abraham. "The Journeys of James Needham and James Arthur." August 22, 1774. Letter deposited in the Shaftesbury Papers, Public Record Office of London, England. Original eighteenth-century text in *The First Explorations of the Trans-Allegheny Region by the Virginians, 1650–1674*, edited by Clarence Walworth Alvord and Lee Bidgood. Cleveland, OH: The Arthur H. Clark Company, 1912. Modern text in *Early Travels in the Tennessee Country, 1540–1800*, edited by Samuel Cole Williams. Johnson City, TN: The Watauga Press, 1928, and as "The Travels of James Needham and Gabriel Arthur through Virginia, North Carolina, and Beyond, 1673–1674," edited by R.P. Stephen Davis Jr. *Southern Indian Studies* 39 (1990). Davis text online at the University of North Carolina at Chapel Hill's "Research Laboratories of Archaeology" in both original seventeenth-century and edited modern language formats—http://rla.unc.edu/archives/accounts/Needham/Needham.html. (The Davis-edited text is followed in this anthology.)

Zeigler, Wilbur G., and Ben S. Grosscup. *The Heart of the Alleghanies or Western North Carolina: Comprising Its Topography, History, Resources, People, Narratives, Incidents, and Pictures of Travel, Adventures in Hunting and Fishing, and Legends of Its Wilderness.* Raleigh, NC: Alfred Williams, and Cleveland, OH: W.W. Williams, 1883. Reissued (hardcover and softcover "quick print" editions) Kila, MT: Kessinger Publishing Company ("Legacy Reprint Series"), 2007. Online at D.H. Ramsey Library, Special Collections, University of North Carolina at Asheville—http://toto.lib.unca.edu/findingaids/books/zeigler/default_zeigler.htm.

Secondary Sources

(Note that *American National Biography Online* is available by subscription—but it can also be accessed via the databases at many university and municipal libraries. Some libraries also provide the twenty-four-volume print edition: *American National Biography*, John A. Garraty and Mark C. Carnes, general eds., New York: Oxford University Press, 1999.)

Anon. "Wilbur G. Zeigler." *The Bay of San Francisco* 2. Chicago: Lewis Publishing Co., 1892. Online at "San Francisco County Biographies"—http://freepages.genealogy.rootsweb.com/~npmelton/sfbzeig.htm.

———. "Wilbur G. Zeigler." *The Builders of a Great City: San Francisco's Representative Men.* Vol. 1 of 2. San Francisco: San Francisco Journal of Commerce Publishing Co., 1891. Online at "Google Book Search—http://books.google.com/books?hl=en&id=nh8NAAAAIAAJ&dq=%22the+builders+of+a+great+city%22&printsec=frontcover&source=web&ots=ZlUAiq8iSq&sig=DvYpYPRyIBTB4swt9QrIfBEsItM.

————. "Wilbur G. Zeigler." *History of Sandusky County, Ohio, with Portraits and Biographies of Prominent Citizens and Pioneers.* Cleveland, OH: H.Z. Williams & Bro., 1882. Online at "Heritage Pursuit"—http://www.heritagepursuit.com/Sandusky/SanduskyIndex.htm.

Arthur, John Preston. *Western North Carolina: A History (from 1730 to 1913).* Asheville, NC: Edward Buncombe Chapter of the Daughters of the American Revolution, 1914. Reissued Johnson City, TN: The Overmountain Press, 1966.

Atwood, Wallace W. *The Physiographic Provinces of North America.* Boston: Ginn and Company, 1940.

Becker, Kate Harbes. *Biography of Christian Reid.* Belmont, NC: self-published, 1941.

Branch, Michael P., and Daniel J. Philippon, eds. *Nature Writing from Virginia's Blue Ridge Mountains and Shenandoah Valley.* Baltimore, MD: Johns Hopkins University Press, 1998.

Brewster, William. "An Ornithological Reconnaissance in Western North Carolina," *The Auk* 3. 1886.

Briceland, Alan Vance. "Abraham Wood." 2000. *American National Biography Online*—http://www.anb.org/articles/01/01-01005.html.

————. *Westward from Virginia: The Exploration of the Virginia-Carolina Frontier, 1650–1710.* Charlottesville: University of Virginia Press, 1987.

Brooks, Maurice. *The Appalachians.* Boston: Houghton Mifflin Co., 1965.

Brown, Claud A., and L. Katherine Kirkman. *Trees of Georgia and Adjacent States.* Portland, OR: Timber Press, 1990.

Byer, Fred. *North Carolina: The Years Before Man—A Geologic History.* Durham, NC: Carolina Academic Press, 1991.

Byrd, William. "History of the Dividing Line Run in the Year 1728." In *William Byrd's Histories of the Dividing Line Betwixt Virginia and North Carolina.* Raleigh: North Carolina Historical Commission, 1929.

Cairns, John S. *List of the Birds of Buncombe County, North Carolina.* Weaverville, NC: self-published, 1891.

———. "The Summer Birds of Buncombe County, North Carolina." *Ornithologist and Oologist* 14 (February 1889).

Clingman, Thomas Lanier. "Mount Pisgah, North Carolina." *Appletons' Journal* 10 (December 1873). Collected in *Selections From the Speeches and Writings of Thomas Lanier Clingman*. Raleigh, NC: John Nichols, 1877.

Colton, Henry E., and George Stephens. "Henry Elliott Colton." *Dictionary of North Carolina Biography* 1. Edited by William S. Powell. Chapel Hill: University of North Carolina, 1979. (One of the coauthors of this article was perhaps a descendant of Henry Elliott Colton?)

Congleton, Donna. "Frances Christine Fisher Tiernan." 2000. *American National Biography Online*—http://www.anb.org/articles/16/16-01643.html.

Dillon, Richard. "John Muir." 2000. *American National Biography Online*—http://www.anb.org/articles/20/20-00697.html.

Ellison, George. *Mountain Passages: Natural and Cultural History of Western North Carolina and the Great Smoky Mountains*. Charleston, SC: The History Press, 2005.

Ellison, George, and Elizabeth Ellison. *Blue Ridge Nature Journal: Reflections on the Appalachian Mountains in Essays and Art*. Charleston, SC: The Natural History Press, 2006. Reissued, in part, as *Blue Ridge Nature Notes: Selections from Blue Ridge Nature Journal*. Charleston, SC: The Natural History Press, 2007.

Ellison-Murphree, M.L. Shared research relevant to Wilbur G. Zeigler and Ben S. Grosscup's stay in Western North Carolina, Zeigler's newspaper contributions and the composition of *The Heart of the Alleghanies*.

Erlich, Gretel. *John Muir: Nature's Visionary*. Washington, D.C.: National Geographic, 2000.

Fenneman, Nevin M. *Physiography of Eastern United States*. New York: McGraw-Hill Book Company, Inc., 1938.

Fields, Mrs. James T. *Charles Dudley Warner*. New York: McClure, Phillips & Co., 1904.

Fink, Paul, and Myron H. Avery. "Arnold Guyot's Explorations in the Great Smoky Mountains." *Appalachia* (December 1936).

Fradkin, Arlene. *Cherokee Folk Zoology: The Animal World of a Native American People, 1700–1838*. New York: Garland Publishing, Inc., 1990.

Freel, Margaret Walker. *Our Heritage: The People of Cherokee County, North Carolina, 1540–1955*. Asheville, NC: Miller Printing Co., 1956.

Frome, Michael. *Strangers in High Places: The Story of the Great Smoky Mountains*. Expanded edition. Knoxville: University of Tennessee Press, 1994.

Gale, Robert L. "Charles Dudley Warner." 2000. *American National Biography Online*—http://www.anb.org/articles/16/16-0172.html.

Gibbons, Felton, and Deborah Storm. *Neighbors to the Birds: A History of Birdwatching in America*. New York: W.W. Norton & Company, 1988.

Houk, Rose. *Great Smoky Mountains National Park: A Natural History Guide*. Boston: Houghton Mifflin Company, 1993.

Hudson, Charles. *Knights of Spain, Warriors of the Sun: Hernando de Soto and the South's Ancient Chiefdoms*. Athens: University of Georgia Press, 1997.

———. *The Southeastern Indians*. Knoxville: University of Tennessee Press, 1976.

———. "Uktena: A Cherokee Anomalous Monster." *Journal of Cherokee Studies* 3 (Spring 1978).

Hunt, Charles B. *Natural Regions of the United States and Canada*. San Francisco: W.H. Freeman and Company, 1974.

Inscoe, John. "John Lyon." *Dictionary of North Carolina Biography* 4. Edited by William S. Powell. Chapel Hill: University of North Carolina Press, 1991.

Jeffrey, Thomas E. "Thomas Lanier Clingman." 2000. *American National Biography Online*—http://www.anb.org/articles/20/20-00697.html.

Jennings, Francis. "James Adair." 2000. *American National Biography Online*—http://www.anb.org/articles/16/16-0172.html.

Kastner, Joseph. *A Species of Eternity*. New York: E.P. Dutton, 1969.

Kearney, H. Thomas, Jr. "Thomas Lanier Clingman." *Dictionary of North Carolina Biography* 1. Edited by William S. Powell. Chapel Hill: University of North Carolina Press, 1979.

"Lanman, Charles." *The Dictionary of American Biography* 10. London: Oxford University Press, 1960.

Laughlin, Jennifer. *Roan Mountain: A Passage of Time.* Johnson City, TN: The Overmountain Press, 1999.

Loudon, John. *Arboretum et Fruticum Brittanicum.* London: printed for the author, 1838.

McNeil, W.K., ed. *Appalachian Images in Folk and Popular Culture.* Ann Arbor: University of Michigan Research Press, 1989. Reissued Knoxville: University of Tennessee Press, 1995.

McPhail, Ian. "André Michaux." 2000. *American National Biography Online*—http://www.anb.org/articles/16/16-0172.html.

Newhouse, Thomas. "Edward Smith King." 2000. *American National Biography Online*—http://www.anb.org/articles/16/16-00913.html.

O'Donnell, Kevin E. "Bradford Torrey (1843–1912)." *Early American Nature Writers: A Biographical Encyclopedia.* Edited by Daniel Patterson, et al. Westport, CT: Greenwood Press, 2007.

O'Donnell, Kevin E., and Helen Hollingsworth, eds. *Seekers of Scenery: Travel Writing from Southern Appalachia (1840–1900).* Knoxville: University of Tennessee Press, 2004.

Powell, William S. *The North Carolina Gazetteer: A Dictionary of Tar Heel Places.* Chapel Hill: University of North Carolina Press, 1968.

Queen, Louise L. "Augustus Gottlieb Spangenberg." *Dictionary of North Carolina Biography* 5. Edited by William S. Powell. Chapel Hill: University of North Carolina Press, 1994.

Rankin, Richard, ed. *North Carolina Nature Writing: Four Centuries of Personal Narratives and Descriptions.* Winston-Salem, NC: John F. Blair, Publisher, 1996.

Roe, Charles E. *A Directory to North Carolina's Natural Areas.* Raleigh: North Carolina Natural Heritage Foundation, 1987.

Savage, Henry, Jr. *Lost Heritage.* New York: William Morrow and Company, Inc., 1970.

Savage, Henry, Jr., and Elizabeth J. Savage. *André and Francois André Michaux.* Charlottesville: University Press of Virginia, 1986.

Schwarzkopf, S. Kent. *A History of Mount Mitchell and the Black Mountains: Exploration, Development, and Preservation.* Raleigh: North Carolina Division of Archives and History, 1985.

Shaffner, Randolph P. *Heart of the Blue Ridge: Highlands, North Carolina*. Highlands, NC: Faraway Publishing, 2001.

Silver, Timothy. *Mount Mitchell and the Black Mountains: An Environmental History of the Highest Peaks in Eastern America*. Chapel Hill: University of North Carolina Press, 2003.

Simpson, Marcus B., Jr. *Birds of the Blue Ridge Mountains*. Chapel Hill: University of North Carolina Press, 1992.

———. "John S. Cairns." 2000. *American National Biography Online*—http://www.anb.org/articles/13-00191.html.

———. "John S. Cairns." *Dictionary of North Carolina Biography* 1. Edited by William S. Powell. Chapel Hill: University of North Carolina Press, 1979.

———."William Brewster." 2000. *American National Biography Online*—http://www.anb.org/articles/13-00191.html.

Smith, Gary Scott. "Arnold Henry Guyot." 2000. *American National Biography Online*—http://www.anb.org/articles/13/13-00673.html.

Smith, Maud Thomas. "James Robert Adair." *Dictionary of North Carolina Biography* 1. Edited by William S. Powell. Chapel Hill: University of North Carolina, 1979.

Sondley, F.A. *A History of Buncombe County, North Carolina*. 2 vols. Asheville, NC: The Advocate Printing Co., 1930.

Spongberg, Stephen A. *A Reunion of Trees: The Discovery of Exotic Plants and Their Introduction into North American and European Landscapes*. Cambridge, MA: Harvard University Press, 1990.

Stevenson, George. "John Strother." *Dictionary of North Carolina Biography* 5. Edited by William S. Powell. Chapel Hill: University of North Carolina, 1979.

Stupka, Arthur. *Notes on the Birds of Great Smoky Mountains National Park*. Knoxville: University of Tennessee Press, 1963.

Swanson, Robert E. *A Field Guide to the Trees and Shrubs of the Southern Appalachians*. Baltimore, MD: Johns Hopkins University Press, 1994.

Taylor, David, ed. *South Carolina Naturalists: An Anthology, 1700–1860*. Columbia: University of South Carolina Press, 1998.

Webster, William David, et al. *Mammals of the Carolinas, Virginia and Maryland*. Chapel Hill: University of North Carolina Press, 1985.

Weidensaul, Scott. *Mountains of the Heart: A Natural History of the Appalachians*. Golden, CO: Fulcrum Publishing, 1994.

Wessel, Carola. "Augustus Gottlieb Spangenberg." 2000. *American National Biography Online*—http://www.anb.org/articles/01/01-00846.html.

Wise, Kenneth, and Ron Peterson. *A Natural History of Mount Le Conte*. Knoxville: University of Tennessee Press, 1998.

Wofford, B. Eugene. *Guide to the Vascular Plants of the Blue Ridge*. Athens: University of Georgia Press, 1989.

———, director. University of Tennessee Herbarium. Online at—http://tenn.bio.utk.edu/vascular/vascular.html.

Zeigler, Wilbur G. *It was Marlowe: A Story of the Secret of Three Centuries*. Chicago: Donohue, Henneberry & Co., 1895.

———. *Story of the Earthquake and Fire*. San Francisco: L.C. Osteyee, 1906.

ABOUT THE EDITOR AND ILLUSTRATOR

George and Elizabeth Ellison moved to Western North Carolina in 1973. His office is situated at Elizabeth Ellison Watercolors, a gallery-studio Elizabeth owns and operates on the town square in Bryson City. Since 1976, they have made their home in a forty-six-acre cove surrounded on three sides by the Great Smoky Mountains National Park.

George wrote the biographical introductions for the reissues of two southern Appalachian classics: Horace Kephart's *Our Southern Highlanders* (University of Tennessee Press, 1976) and James Mooney's *Myths of the Cherokees* (Historical Images, 1992). He writes the "Nature Journal" column for the *Asheville Citizen-Times*, the "Botanical Excursions" column for *Chinquapin: The Newsletter of the Southern Appalachian Botanical Society* and the "Back Then" regional history column for *Smoky Mountain News*. A collection of his essays, *Mountain Passages: Natural and Cultural History of Western North Carolina*, was published in 2005 by The History Press. In 2006, the same press published *A Blue Ridge Nature Journal: Reflections on the Appalachians in Essays and Art*, which includes thirty of George's essays on the natural areas, flora and fauna of the southern mountains, as well as forty full-color watercolors and thirty illustrations by Elizabeth. It was among the finalists of those titles nominated for the SIBA (Southern Independent Booksellers Alliance) nonfiction book of the year award. The History Press also published *Blue Ridge Nature Notes: Selections from Blue Ridge Nature Journal* in 2007. Contact information is available at www.georgeellison.com.

Elizabeth has exhibited and sold her work widely throughout the United States. Utilizing both traditional and oriental techniques, she depicts the varied wildflowers, animals, human inhabitants and landscapes of the Smokies region and beyond. She frequently gathers and processes native Appalachian plants—black willow, mulberry, cattail, papyrus, rush, iris, wisteria, yucca, raspberry, blackberry and more—to make the handmade papers she incorporates into her paintings. Her pen-and-ink drawings and watercolor washes long have graced the work of her husband and other writers. Publishing venues include the *Asheville Citizen-Times*, *Blue Ridge Outdoors*, *Outdoor Traveler*,

Friends of Wildlife: The Journal of the North Carolina Wildlife Federation and *Chinquapin: The Newsletter of the Southern Appalachian Botanical Society*. She is the cover artist for Niche Gardens of Chapel Hill, North Carolina, an award-winning nursery. She was also the real life watercolorist for the character "Alice" in the movie *Songcatcher*, which was filmed in Western North Carolina in 1999. Contact information is available at www.elizabeth ellisonwatercolors.com.

Visit us at
www.historypress.net